T0033179

# CARIS SNIDER

## Car Line MOM
### DEVOTIONAL

**100 Days of Encouragement**

for the Mama Who Gets Everybody Everywhere

**B&H**
PUBLISHING
BRENTWOOD, TENNESSEE

978-1-0877-8077-1

Published by B&H Publishing Group
Brentwood, Tennessee

Dewey Decimal Classification: 242.643
Subject Heading: DEVOTIONAL LITERATURE \ WOMEN \
CHRISTIAN LIFE

All Scripture is taken from the English Standard Version.
ESV® Text Edition: 2016. Copyright © 2001 by Crossway
Bibles, a publishing ministry of Good News Publishers.

Cover design by Jennifer Allison/513 TN. Illustration by
ProStock-Studio/shutterstock. Lettering by Trigubova Irina/
shutterstock. Author photo by Joelle Brooks Photography.

1 2 3 4 5 6 • 26 25 24 23

*To all of the moms in this season of car line life, I dedicate this book to you. Being on this journey with you has my heart filled with excitement and anticipation to see how God will move in your life.*

# **Acknowledgments**

Without a team who believes in your vision and the words you present, a book cannot be created. *Car Line Mom* would not be here if it were not for the amazing team at B&H. To my editors, Ashley and Clarissa, your notes and touches on each page has made room for God's Word to permeate every mama heart as she reads each day. Brandon, Zoe, and Allye, you have encouraged me to walk in this calling God has placed on my life; thank you. I love you!

To Del Duduit, my agent, thank you for challenging me and believing in me.

To my coach, Alli, your push to finish the proposal was exactly what I needed.

Finally, to my church family, who has been so supportive of this writing journey. You will never know how much your prayers, texts, and encouraging words have carried me through.

# Contents

# Introduction

Hello, fellow mama! I'm Caris Snider, and I'm a mom of two kids, sitting right alongside you in this "car line" season of parenthood, trying to make sure I not only remember Jesus each day, but packing all the lunches too! Sound familiar?

Before you read one day of this devotional, or reheat your third cup of coffee, know this . . . the time you are investing in this car line season is not wasted. Jesus is calling out to you in the midst of the mundane and constant hustle. He has a potent dose of *truth* prepared to speak to your heart over the next 100 days. You will gain joy as you laugh along with relatable stories. You will discover new strategies to focus your thoughts with a heavenly perspective. The shame and guilt holding you down on the bathroom floor will be scrubbed away with His marvelous grace. God's Word will come alive as you sit in your favorite chair or park next to the laughter of tiny voices to see what each new day will bring.

I want to encourage you to mark each page with your flair pens or even stain them with your mascara tears. *You are not alone* in this span of time, my friend. Shall we flip the page together and begin?

All my love,
Caris

DAY 1

# Hectic Mornings,
# Chaotic Afternoons

*But for me it is good to be near God; I have made
the Lord GOD my refuge, that I may tell of all your works.*
PSALM 73:28

To all my fellow car line moms, I have discovered we are not alone in our afflictions in this season of coming and going. Trying to find space to breathe and a rhythm to move toward our heavenly Father seems daunting at times for all of us. The hectic scene of a morning filled with tears, screams, and messes . . . then the kids wake up and it's their turn. To the afternoon chaos of all the activities, all the guilt of another fast-food meal, and all the shame of feeling like a failure one more day.

Our souls long for the presence of God, but how do we get there? My prayer, as we journey through these next few weeks together, is that He will peel the curtain back for us one layer at a time. He desires for us to incline in His presence, and I believe He will reveal to each one of us every baby step.

Distractions will come and destruction will rear its ugly head as you commit to spending daily time with Him. Give yourself grace just as He will give you. Find the few minutes when you can. It may be sitting on the potty or in your cozy bed, or if you are like me, it will be a warm cup of goodness in your favorite chair.

It is good to be near to God. You don't have to be all cleaned up before you get there. You don't have to wipe the sticky cinnamon rolls off, nor do you have to figure out how to wipe your heart clean on your own. There is no organic cleaner that can do what His presence can.

He does all of that. He does all the cleaning, all the healing, all the restoring. He knows what we need and that we cannot do it for ourselves.

He sees us. He loves us. He is beckoning us into His presence.

## Action Step

You already took an action step sitting in His presence today. Celebrate your victory step!

## Prayer

Dear God, I long to be in Your presence. Holy Spirit, help me to make this priority of spending time with my heavenly Father a nonnegotiable. Amen.

# Did You See That Cow?

*Let your eyes look directly forward, and your gaze be straight before you. Ponder the path of your feet; then all your ways will be sure. Do not swerve to the right or to the left; turn your foot away from evil.*

PROVERBS 4:25–27

"Mom! Did you see that cow?"

This was not a sentence I expected to hear from my daughter as we were moving through the first-grade car line. She likes to play jokes on me, so I decided to go along. I looked over to my right, and there it was . . . a cow beside the row of cars! The stopping and going had been part of our lives for years, but a roaming farm animal was a first. Eye contact was made through the chewed cud, and laughter filled the backseat.

I got distracted and stopped moving. You all know, halting the flow of traffic is not good for morning drop-off. A horn honked and got my focus back on the path in front of me.

The enemy likes to use distractions. He does not want you or me walking in the gifts and calling God has placed on us. Satan knows we are here to spread the good news of the gospel. If he can keep us off track, he will use whatever he can to stop us.

How do we keep our hearts and minds focused on the Lord?

Our verse reminds us to keep our gaze fixed straight ahead. There may be shiny trinkets glistening in the corner of your eye, but they are not as they appear. By having daily time in God's Word, it allows your thoughts to be on Him first. This keeps the action of your feet away from wicked interruptions.

## Action Step

Write this Scripture on a sticky note or piece of paper. Place it on your dashboard as a reminder to keep your vision focused on the Lord.

## Prayer

Lord, help me to keep my thoughts and actions on You and not allow distractions to get me off track. Amen.

# Coffee after Drop-off?

*Therefore encourage one another and build
one another up, just as you are doing.*
1 THESSALONIANS 5:11

*"Coffee after drop-off?"*

Hearing the phone ding in the morning chaos can add another level of irritation, but seeing a happy message changes my attitude in an instant. A friend had no idea how much I needed this escape she offered in the early hours. Gathering with her at the local coffeehouse over a warm cup of conversation was exactly what my soul needed.

Have you ever found yourself in this place, in the midst of the morning hustle five days a week? It begins to pile on, and life is so busy you forget to pause and unpack all the overwhelming things. The schedule pushes you into isolation when you really need community.

Encouraging one another gives unspoken permission to lean on others. Oftentimes we are scared to ask for help or say we need to talk. Offering an uplifting word or asking someone to go talk gives freedom to bear the soul.

Don't push away inviting a friend on a walk or grabbing a meal as a silly notion. This could be the Holy Spirit giving you a gentle nudge to lift up a friend, or for you to invite a load-bearer into the trenches of your life.

## *Action Step*

Who is a friend you can reach out to and invite
into your space today? Is this someone who needs
a pick-me-up or someone who can help pick you up?
Give coffee or a meal a try and see what happens.

## *Prayer*

Dear Lord, thank You for giving us friendship and reminding
us of the importance of an encouraging word. Amen.

# Fear of the Cone

*God is our refuge and strength,*
*a very present help in trouble.*
PSALM 46:1

Where I live, the orange cone is infamous. If you arrive one minute after the warning bell rings, it makes an appearance. No car can pass. Your child cannot walk in unattended. You must get out of the car and sign them in. Of course, this always happens when you don't have an appointment to attend or work to complete in person, so getting ready is not part of your morning. I always feared this cone, but somehow I made it without ever facing the doom it gave out to anyone daring to challenge it.

Being late for drop-off is a legitimate fear. No one wants to be seen in their hole-y pajamas, make-up-less face, lack of support, or morning breath unhinged!

What do you do when trouble drops right in your path, bringing you to a halt?

God wants us to turn to Him in difficult times. By being present, this means He is right there. Not only is He right there, but He's always there. The Lord's help is a permanent fixture, and His presence will be constant with no ebb or flow.

The refuge He freely gives allows us to discover deliverance only He can provide in a troublesome situation.

The orange cone of life may be an unwelcoming interruption for you in this season, but allow it to pivot you into the arms of your Defender.

## Action Step

What is the orange cone in your life right now?
Confess it to the Lord, and allow Him to be a hiding place
for you while His presence renews your strength.

## Prayer

Dear Lord, thank You for always being there. Knowing I can
come to You with the good, the bad, and the ugly gives my
soul respite. Amen.

# DAY 5

# Ugly Crying

*You make known to me the path of life; in your presence there is fullness of joy; at your right hand are pleasures forevermore.*
PSALM 16:11

It was a chocolate kind of day.

As I drove up to my space in line for the afternoon, I couldn't wait to sit in the inactivity. Food wrappers, shoes, and clothes surrounded me physically, but God's presence surrounded me spiritually. Worship music filled the sound waves, declaring the name of Jesus over fear, anxiety, and depression. I couldn't bite my lip hard enough to keep the river of tears from streaming down my face.

The ugly cry was in full-blown effect. Shoulders shaking and lips quivering. My big sunglasses could not hide the brokenness that day.

There is something therapeutic about an ugly cry. All the hidden places are revealed and washed clean. God comes in with His glory leaving behind peace.

When was the last time you allowed the tears to flow? When you sat in God's presence and allowed Him to love on you with all the fullness of joy He brings?

You are right where you need to be in this car line of life. God's path for you goes through the waiting and the going. There is nothing wrong with taking these moments to:

Pause.

Weep.

Worship.

This surrendered time allows God's spirit to overflow and refresh your soul.

## Action Step

Don't hold your tears anymore. Loosen your grip
and invite the Holy Spirit into the river ready
to flow and wash you in His presence.

## Prayer

Dear Lord, thank You for allowing me to blubber my praises
to You. Your loving kindness toward me gives freedom to
express myself in a way I never knew possible. Amen.

# Now What Do I Do?

*For we are his workmanship, created in Christ Jesus
for good works, which God prepared beforehand,
that we should walk in them.*
EPHESIANS 2:10

Have you ever driven away in tears?

They smile and wave good-bye, walking in with their group of friends, and you disappear in the silence of an empty minivan. For some reason, everything hits different. The garage door goes up, and you don't know how you arrived home. Mascara is running down your face while laundry waits on the dining room table.

*"Now what do I do?"*

As moms, it is very easy to connect our purpose to all we do for our children. When the doing stops, it becomes simple to get caught in the trap of thinking we have lost our purpose. Tying shoes, wiping noses, and cleaning boo-boos are important work, but it is not all you are equipped to do.

God placed more in you while weaving you together. Not only is there more good works, there is grace.

Sitting in His grace is an important action to take before any other. Seizing this moment to sit at the feet of Jesus and move out of paralysis into a calm stillness will change your perspective.

Once grace has permeated your heart, the good works are revealed to you, His masterpiece, to complete. In some translations, *masterpiece* is used in this passage instead of *workmanship*. A masterpiece is a one-of-a-kind piece of art. It cannot be duplicated or matched in its splendor.

God knitted you. He took time creating you, hammering gifts and talents in you unlike anyone else.

When your children go off to school, this doesn't mean you are finished. Your job is shifting in task. When you drop them off, it's not the end. It is the beginning of new ways to serve and love on this world.

### Action Step

List things you enjoy doing. Add gifts and talents
others have pointed out in you. Circle one to search
for more ways to use in your life.

### Prayer

God, help me to remember I am a masterpiece in Your eyes.
Help me to use the gifts You have given me to serve others.
Thank You, Lord, for not being done with me. Amen.

# Tuck, Roll, and Go!

*The LORD said to Moses, "Why do you cry to me? Tell the
people of Israel to go forward. Lift up your staff, and stretch
out your hand over the sea and divide it, that the people of
Israel may go through the sea on dry ground."*
EXODUS 14:15–16

All of our hugs, kisses, and awesome-day wishes happen before
arriving to car line. We get all of this done so everyone is fixated
on the exit out of the car. Backpacks zipped, lunch boxes in
hand, and eyes focused. Once we slow down by the awning,
it's time . . . tuck, roll, and go!

I jokingly told my girls to do this one day because the cars
in front of us were not moving. They were at a standstill. Kids
were being peeled off the seat and shoes were still being tied.
Jitters took over in these vehicles at the thought of what was
ahead for the day. No one was ready. Instead, fear had taken
over and forward progress stopped.

This is where we find the Israelites in today's passage.
Terror has gripped the masses and paralyzed them from any
motion.

They saw themselves trapped by a huge body of water
and an army of men and chariots. It appeared there was
nowhere to go, and the Israelites began to complain, wanting
to go back to Egypt. Back to slavery. Back to what was familiar.

God needed them to move forward in faith. Yes, it may have looked one way, but He was with them, and they could believe and trust in Him.

As this story continues, we read the miraculous way of how God took them on dry ground to the other side. Not one person was left behind. Their heavenly Father brought deliverance right on time and revealed His mighty power.

Is God asking you to move forward? Is fear paralyzing you, trying to force you back into what feels familiar?

God has got you. He does not change. His ability to lead the Israelites through a raging sea is there for you. Instead of looking at your inability, look to His unwavering faithfulness. Then, take one step, then the next, and the next. He did not call you out of Egypt to leave you stranded.

## Action Step

Face your fear today. Choose one small step you can take to catapult you to a giant leap of faith.

## Prayer

Dear Lord, thank You for reminding me of Your faithfulness in my life. If You can lead the Israelites to dry ground, You can do the same for me. I am stepping out in faith, trusting in You. Amen.

# The Everything Table

*And let us consider how to stir up one another
to love and good works, not neglecting to meet together,
as is the habit of some, but encouraging one another,
and all the more as you see the Day drawing near.*
HEBREWS 10:24–25

I see her table as I pass the bay window and stop sign. I don't know this fellow mama, but I believe we would be best friends if I did. This gathering place looks much like mine. It can go from a meal of laughter and full bellies, to a bottomless pit of socks with no match, to the homework project going on past midnight because it is due in a few hours.

Every time I drive by, I look to my left to see what this bay window will display. As I look at that table, I relate to it and recline back in my spirit knowing I'm not alone as other mamas fill their tables. Celebrations of another year around the sun, heated arguments where tears and red faces emerge. Bibles with wrinkled pages from the prayers of a broken-hearted parent traipsing through a jungle of the unknown.

Find another table like yours. There is no judgment when you pull out the chair. Be the everything table for another mom who thinks her house, her heart, her life are the only ones with all the different piles.

## Action Step 🌮

Share your everything table. You have no idea
who needs to know someone out there gets it.

## Prayer

Dear God, help me to encourage and love on my fellow mama
friends. We need each other's tables. Amen.

# Not a Baby Anymore

*Train up a child in the way he should go; even when*
*he is old he will not depart from it.*
PROVERBS 22:6

Long before you cradled your babies close, God was holding them.

He gave us these children for a season. As they are in our care, we have the opportunity to teach, equip, and prepare them for this world by instructing them on the tools needed to stand strong against the attacks of the enemy.

We are raising warriors!

They are not babies anymore. Preparing them for battle is important. By doing this, we are planting seeds where the world would much rather plant weeds of destruction. How much better will this young generation be as adults if boldness is instilled in them now?

How can we prepare our warriors for battle when the urge comes to overprotect and shield them from the arrows always flying in their direction from the devil?

Start with the master blueprint God gave through the Bible. Read His Word together. Take daily time to pray with one another. Instill the importance of being involved in the local church. Discover ways you can serve the community as a family. Have conversation about how to share the love of Jesus with others.

Sit with them in the hard things, and guide their gaze to the Lord in those junctures of life. Help your children to seek God's answer instead of the world's perversion of truth.

Remember, training is an ongoing process. There will be intervals of time you may not get it right. God's grace is sufficient in those moments. He is not asking you to parent in perfection. He is asking you to parent in obedience. He will take care of the rest.

## Action Step

Pick one way you will begin equipping
your warriors, and write it down.

## Prayer

God, help me to remember You have called me to
train up the tiny human beings You have put in my care.
I want Your warriors to be prepared for battle with
the equipment You have freely given. Amen.

# Are You Sure This Is the Right Way?

*The LORD said to Abraham, "Why did Sarah laugh and say, 'Shall I indeed bear a child, now that I am old?' Is anything too hard for the LORD? At the appointed time I will return to you, about this time next year, and Sarah shall have a son."*
GENESIS 18:13–14

My husband wanted to ride with me for car line one afternoon. I tried to prepare him for the quick turns, slammed brakes, and multiple shifts in direction to get to our desired locations.

Let's just say he didn't believe me.

As I weaved quickly, but safely, through the first car line, the only thing I could tell him was, "Hold on."

There is a straight path leading to the elementary school, but when it comes to afternoon pick-up, each grade has a different location. For those who normally do not go that path, it feels wrong. He could not understand how all the twists and turns would get us to our set destination.

I felt comfortable in all the shifting, but he had the deer in the headlights look: *"Are you sure this is the right way?!"*

He had to trust me. I knew this route like the back of my hand. Even though the process felt strange to him, once we got to where we needed to be, it all made sense.

God works in our lives the same way. We find ourselves doubting the curves and getting confused about the rough places, wanting to ask Him, "Are You sure this is the right way, Lord?"

Have you ever asked this when the road takes a turn or goes a different way, leading you out of your comfort zone?

Sarah laughed when God said she would have a baby. Now, let's be honest—can you see where she is coming from? I know I can. If I were eighty-nine years old and an angel told me this, I think I would laugh or faint in shock! This is not what she expected, but God delivered.

Nothing is too hard for Him. Hold on to the promise He gave you. Your path may have been difficult, but God knows where He is guiding you. It is not like our Good Father to say He will do something and not do it.

If He said it, He will do it.

## Action Step

What hard thing has God revealed He wants to do in your life? What small faith step has He asked you to take in your winding journey to this destination? Take it today.

## Prayer

I have to confess my doubt in the way You have led me on this path, Lord. Forgive me for thinking You have no idea where to go. Help me to trust the plan and take this next step of faith.
Amen.

# Cutting Out Squares

*"For even the Son of Man came not to be served but to serve, and to give his life as a ransom for many."*
MARK 10:45

Kindergarten teachers are my heroes! They are on the front line of training boys and girls how to do basic skills needed over the next twelve years of life. They are tasked with making learning fun while hitting all the benchmarks. These creative minds put wonderful projects in place to give children an opportunity to learn in the style fitting them best. All of these ideas require a multitude of pieces.

One of our kindergarten teachers put math facts on colored paper for her students to use for practice at home. Twenty students require lots of tiny squares! As parents, she invited us into her process to help pass our time in the afternoon car line. We could cut these squares out for her, allowing the small amount of time she had to be used in a valuable way.

Serving her and the children granted us permission to not feel as though our time in line was wasted. It became moments of service.

Jesus gives us a beautiful picture of servanthood when He washed the feet of the disciples at the Last Supper. This was a humbling act, and the disciples were not quite sure how to respond. Here is the Son of God cleaning their feet when they felt the roles needed to be reversed.

How can you serve the teachers washing the feet of your children? Are there activities you can volunteer to attend? Do they have items needing ends cut and trimmed? What prayers can you lift up on behalf of the educator God has placed into your family's path?

However He leads you to serve, know what seems small to you will bring big impact for them.

## Action Step

Find one way to serve your child's teacher this week.

## Prayer

Dear Jesus, I want to follow Your example and wash the feet of the teachers You have placed in the lives of my children. Amen.

# Still in Pajamas

*Do not speak evil against one another, brothers. The one who
speaks against a brother or judges his brother, speaks evil
against the law and judges the law. But if you judge the law,
you are not a doer of the law but a judge. There is only one
lawgiver and judge, he who is able to save and to destroy.
But who are you to judge your neighbor?*

JAMES 4:11–12

Raise your hand if you have ever gone in the car line with your
pajamas still on.

Now that we all have our hands in the air, breathe a sigh
of relief. We have all been there, done that, and will probably
do it again tomorrow.

Confession . . . I have also been on the other side in judging the disheveled mom who gets out of her car with pajamas
still on, messy hair bun, and fuzzy animal slippers. Allowing my
thoughts to go to a negative place about her is not something
I am proud to admit, but I have been there.

In those moments, the Holy Spirit brings conviction with
questions: Do you know what she has been through this morning? Do you know if her home life is happy or stressful? Do you
know if her kids listened or gave her a hard time today? Do
you know if she has been struggling mentally and it is a huge
victory for her to be out of bed taking her kids to school?

Ouch.

We have no idea what other moms around us are facing and the struggles they hide behind their smiles. Faking it until we make is something we can all find common ground on in different circumstances of life.

By remembering we are not the judge, we can be the friend. The relationship will be different in all situations, but it can always be based on maintaining a judgment-free zone. A safe place we would want for ourselves.

The next time you see someone riding high in their pajamas, give a salute and let them know you are with them and praying for them.

## Action Step

Reach out to a mom you are getting to know. Ask how you can pray over her. Give space for a transparent response to allow God's love to hug her heart.

## Prayer

Thank You, God, for allowing me to come as I am in Your presence. Help me to extend this same grace to other women You have placed in my path. Amen.

# From Kindergarten to the Middle School Dance

*The LORD will keep your going out and your coming in from this time forth and forevermore.*
PSALM 121:8

I will never forget the Sunday my oldest decided to dress herself for church. As always, we were running behind, so I welcomed the help from the tiny hands of my kindergartner. She came out of her bedroom with the biggest grin of accomplishment.

Have you ever had those moments as a mom where you are giggling inside but smiling on the outside with hesitant approval? That is where I found myself. She found her fancy, sparkly blue dress in the back of her closet. The light hit her just right as she spun in the living room. Her feet danced in her only pair of ruffle socks and school tennis shoes. She did not forget her favorite hat with Minnie Mouse's face and ears exploding through the top. It was a sight to see!

Now, she is coming out of her bedroom in another blue dress and white tennis shoes with a hint of makeup and silky-smooth hair.

The comings and goings in this life pass by more quickly than you can imagine pre-parenting. Daily tasks become daunting, and precious moments can be hard to snag. Yet, God reminds us that He keeps our every juncture before Him.

Have you found yourself wondering if God is truly interested in how your day-to-day goes? Allow today's passage to be the gentle reminder your soul needs. He cares about every part of your life. He wants all of you so He can be in all of the minutes and the moments.

## Action Step

Practice talking to God about the little things on your schedule today. Allow yourself to let this Scripture permeate every part of your coming and going.

## Prayer

Dear Lord, I needed this reminder today. Thank You for caring about all of my life, big and small. Amen.

# Bump in the Road Equals Coffee on Clothes

*And we know that for those who love God all
things work together for good, for those who
are called according to his purpose.*
ROMANS 8:28

It never fails. Every time I take my glorious cup of coffee with me
to drop my kids off for school, I hit the bump in the road in front
of our driveway. There can be one sip left or a limitless supply,
and out it comes. All over me and my seat. My kids never know
if it is okay to laugh or if they should cry along.

This warm mug of delight has now become cold with tears
filling the inside. It's as if this one bump messed up everything,
bringing all the hidden brokenness to the surface. The scenarios of unfulfilled moments flash before your eyes. The mistakes
looming in your mind are puddled on the floorboard beneath
your feet. Devastating losses come sneaking back into your
thoughts, and you believe this is how life is destined to be.

Or so it appears.

God wastes nothing. The coffee sitting on your floorboard
is not wasted. The job lost is not wasted. The marriage struggle you are going through is not wasted. The prodigal child is
not wasted. Your battle with depression is not wasted.

God will use it all for good. Bumps in your journey are opportunities for God to whisper His love louder. It jolts us to look up and remember He gave us the gift of the Holy Spirit to help in our weakness, as verse 26 mentions in this chapter. He is praying on our behalf when all we can do is weep. When the words don't form, He is already interceding. He knows what we need before we do.

Have you hit a bump, or maybe two, in the road recently? Lean on your friend, the Holy Spirit. Allow Him to comfort you with a tender hug. Sit in His presence, and wait to hear what the silence speaks.

This season is not wasted. God will use it in ways you cannot imagine.

## Action Step

Acknowledge the season you are in.
It could be messy or amazing. Shift your mindset
to see how God is using it for good.

## Prayer

God, I know You can use everything for good in my life. I have
to be honest and confess I am having a hard time seeing it.
Please reveal Your goodness in my messiness. Amen.

# Riding on Empty

*"Come to me, all who labor and are heavy laden,*
*and I will give you rest."*
MATTHEW 11:28

Does anyone else forget to put gas in your car, or is it just me? The light always seems to come on right as car line comes to a screeching halt. One kid is waiting to jump out of the car and go while the other child is panicking, wondering if they will make it to school on time. You are freaking out, pondering if you are going to have to push the car with your 1990 cartoon pajamas on!

If we were being honest, many of us have a habit of pushing our bodies physically and spiritually to empty. Trying to *go go go* and get everything done while the tank gets lower and lower. Finding time to refuel seems unimportant until we run out and become stranded.

God does not want this to happen. He is giving us an invitation in this verse. The first word we see is *come*. He knows we need help. Our Father took the pressure off of us needing to ask Him if we could come, and instead, commanded for us to enter His presence as often as we needed.

How do we refuel? How do we lay down all the heaviness we have carried so long?

We accept His invitation. We abide in His presence. We release control of all the burdens. We come.

## Action Step 📖

Don't wait and put yourself on the back burner any longer. Take it all to God on a regular basis to keep your fuel tank loaded.

## Prayer

God, I need to be refueled in Your presence. Thank You for allowing me to simply come. Amen.

# Thank You, Lord, for Extended Day Workers

> *But he said to me, "My grace is sufficient for you,*
> *for my power is made perfect in weakness." Therefore*
> *I will boast all the more gladly of my weaknesses, so that*
> *the power of Christ may rest upon me.*
> 2 CORINTHIANS 12:9

Can we take a moment of silence to thank the Lord for extended day workers? They help the kids under their care get all homework finished. These employees take them outside to play, releasing pent-up energy. The wonderful men and women who work after hours save us when we fall short in getting the agenda completed.

Work, practice, cleaning the house, getting dinner ready, date night, friend night, small group night . . . and the list goes on. Have people ever asked you how you get all the things done? I think the answer to this is we don't. We have to pick what gets accomplished each day. In the midst of our choosing, we criticize ourselves instead of coming to terms with our fragile humanness.

We were never intended to get all the things done in our own strength.

Breathe easy knowing the expectations we place on ourselves are not from Him. God's grace is a gift in these moments when we think we have failed for not checking off the seventy-five things on the to-do list from dawn to dusk. The Lord could have created the heavens and earth in one day. Instead, He focused on a few important tasks each day. Replace the burden of unrealistic requirements with this example from our heavenly Father.

Self-made lists can be cruel and belittling when we view ourselves from the lack of scratches on a page. Thankfully, God's grace is kind and unending. Shift your gaze from a finite piece of paper to an everlasting reward marked *FINISHED* daily.

## Action Step

When you feel the pressure of not getting all the things done today, inhale grace and exhale the unrealistic expectations.

## Prayer

God, thank You for grace. I struggle with allowing myself to receive something I don't deserve. You know that, and yet You give it to me freely. Help me to follow Your lead. Amen.

# **Stop Rolling to Start Scrolling**

*For am I now seeking the approval of man, or of God?
Or am I trying to please man? If I were still trying
to please man, I would not be a servant of Christ.*
GALATIANS 1:10

Get in line early and for many, the first thing we do is pick up our phone. We go on a mindless scroll binge, and before we know it, the car behind us is waving their arms with frantic motion to move us forward before they go around.

We all get caught in scroll mode.

The dangerous part is when it causes comparison. Inspecting ourselves against others will steal our joy and rob our peace. We take our behind the scenes and measure them against others' highlight reels.

The bed head is not a fair competition against the locks of hair bouncing frizz-free in the wind.

The mom you see with the model-type life feels the same pressure you do to appear one way even though she feels another.

What would happen to us as women if we gave permission to show the behind the scenes? What would happen if we allowed each other to be vulnerable and transparent? How much stronger would we be if we locked arms together and said perfection is not needed to commune at the table together?

Well, here you go. Permission granted. No need to mask what is really happening. No need to hide behind filters and staged shots.

Sharing reality will bring a welcoming sigh of relief to you and the moms in your circle. By you walking freely without the approval of people being the compass to guide your life, they will have courage to do the same.

Seeking to please your heavenly Father is far more rewarding than the praises of people. He has already decided His opinion of you, and it will never be changed.

Your Abba Father loves you now and forever more.

## Action Step 🌮

Instead of scrolling social media while you wait to pick up your children, do a search for all the ways God sees you. For example: You are His child, chosen, loved, His friend, etc.

## Prayer

Dear Lord, thank You for loving me as I am and accepting me into Your embrace. Help me to seek Your applause and not the standing ovations of others. Amen.

# Did You Hear
# the Birds Singing?

*This is the day the LORD has made;*
*let us rejoice and be glad in it.*
PSALM 118:24

The car line may heap stress on your life, but it has potential to breathe in peace.

Some days it is nice to get in line a little early, especially when the sky is crystal clear and the beams of the sun are radiating off the trees. Those minutes when the hint of fall is sneaking in and the air is not filled with humidity—and everyone's hair said amen; those days are kind to us.

In unhindered moments where you can turn your car off, roll the windows down, and listen to the quiet, the song of the birds becomes a beautiful serenade of praise to the Lord.

Gratitude takes over, and the worries of life are gone.

A mind filled with thanksgiving is powerful. Turning our hearts to rejoice in the Lord blocks the anxiety of the day from attacking. It helps us focus on the good. Being in a place of thankfulness keeps us out of the place of anxiousness.

Take time in the car line today. Listen. What beauty do you hear around you? What beauty do you see within you? What beautiful thing can you thank God for today?

## *Action Step* 🌅

An attitude of gratitude is life changing. Consider five things you are thankful for today—write it in your journal or on a sticky note. Throughout your day, challenge yourself to think on other things with thanksgiving and see how differently your day goes.

## *Prayer*

Thank You, Lord, for the natural anxiety blocker You have given me. Help me, Holy Spirit, to lavish my thank-yous on the Good Father today. Amen.

# Less to Full

*"The thief comes only to steal and kill and destroy.
I came that they may have life and have it abundantly."*
JOHN 10:10

It finally happens. You beat the Monday alarm, and the week is off to a phenomenal start! Just the right ratio of coffee to your creamer and your favorite worship songs blasting into your sanctuary of a bathroom. Everything is pleasant until the thoughts come marching in a single-file line:

> *You are WORTHLESS.*
>
> *You are HOPELESS.*
>
> *You are PURPOSELESS.*
>
> *You are USELESS.*

The enemy has entered in with false statements sounding like truth.

In a matter of thirty minutes, your life-giving start comes to a soul-sucking stop. The mascara you thought was water-proof has blackened your face, matching the darkness stream-ing in your heart.

We have all been there, wondering if these lies may be an accurate picture of us.

Thankfully, Jesus knows how to point out a thief. Just as He warned the people in our Scripture to be aware of false prophets and their teachings, He does the same for us. All these fake teachers wanted to do was to bring death and destruction to the lives around them.

Satan is trying to do the same to you. He knows the truth, so his plan is to keep you from discovering it. If you know what Jesus can truly give you, there is no stopping you from running with reckless abandon into His direction.

Jesus gives us a life to experience to the fullest, not just here on earth but in heaven for eternity.

In Him, we are not:

> WORTHLESS but FULL of worth
>
> HOPELESS but HOPEFULL
>
> PURPOSELESS but PURPOSEFULL
>
> USELESS but USEFULL

This is the truth.

The next time you are in FULL motion and those deceptive thoughts try to creep in, hold up your mascara and say, "Not today, you thief! I trust in the One who fills me with His abundant life!"

## Action Step

**Write down these FULL statements
as you cling to God's truth.**

## Prayer

Dear Lord, thank You for loving me to the FULLEST. Help me
to listen to Your truth and not the lies of the enemy. Amen.

# Seriously, I Don't Know What to Do

*". . . We do not know what to do, but our eyes are on you."*
2 CHRONICLES 20:12B

Have you ever found yourself in a moment of not knowing what to do? Your kids have hopped in the car from an afternoon of practice, sharing drama they experienced, and say, "What do I do?" You honestly don't have an answer.

Maybe it is when they sit down at the dinner table to study for a math test they so conveniently informed you would be the next day, and say, "What do I do?" Aware that computing these calculations are beyond what you remember from high school, your response is filled with an echoing, "I don't know."

Or maybe you have found yourself crippled under the weight of fear and anxiety—not sure how to help your tween find those godly friends you desperately long for them to have. You see them come home with sad eyes and a wayward glance. They ask you, "How do I find my friends?" With tears in your eyes the only words you can choke up are, "I don't know."

King Jehoshaphat understood the burden of not knowing what to do. He found himself surrounded by three different enemies, and they were closing in. He didn't pull his army together with all the armor they could find. He didn't tell them his grandiose plans of victory.

Instead, he brought the entire kingdom together—men, women, and children. He stood before this assembly of people and cried out in an honest prayer to God. Prayer was not diminished in his sight. It became the first option instead of the last resort. After praying, they waited on God's response and leading.

Have you found yourself in this place of not knowing what to do? You desperately need an answer, and God is the only one who can give clarity? Follow this powerful example, and go to God in prayer. Cry out to Him. He can handle your frankness. Then, wait. Your knees may be marked with carpet lines, but you will find your life indented with His guiding fingerprint.

## Action Step

Get honest on your knees before the Lord. If you don't know what to do, tell Him. He will meet you where you are.

## Prayer

God, I don't know what to do. I am putting my eyes on You. Thank You that the battle belongs to You, and I can trust Your leading. Amen.

DAY 21

# Praying with Tears

*But Hannah answered, "No, my lord, I am a woman troubled in spirit. I have drunk neither wine nor strong drink, but I have been pouring out my soul before the LORD. Do not regard your servant as a worthless woman, for all along I have been speaking out of my great anxiety and vexation."*

1 SAMUEL 1:15–16

Have you ever found yourself praying with tears? You try to form the words, but the only way they come out is vowels and consonants pooling at your knees. It's a good thing God can read *Cry*.

Hannah was not a mom yet, but her heart was already holding a baby. She desperately wanted a son, but her womb was closed. Her family had gone to the annual celebration at the temple, and she couldn't hold it together any longer. She felt humiliated at the thought of not being able to give Elkanah, her husband, what Peninnah had no trouble conceiving.

She poured her soul out to the Lord. Even though she looked drunk to Eli, the priest, God knew the facts. She could relate to the ache and groaning we have made within our own souls. Hannah leaned into God's presence, communicating in the language of tears.

The Lord met His daughter in her distress. He walked with Hannah through a tumultuous season and opened her

43

womb, allowing her to birth Samuel, who would go on to be an important prophet in the Old Testament.

Are you in anguish over a situation causing you to feel inadequate in your skills as a mom? Do you find yourself looking at other women who seem to not struggle, and yet, you can't put one foot in front of the other?

God is listening to your mama tears. He can breathe life into those barren places you thought were unsalvageable. He placed the name of *Mom* on you knowing your inadequacies full well. That didn't stop Him from choosing you.

If our heavenly Father appointed you to this position, trust He knows what He is doing. Follow Hannah's example, and let your cascade of tears fall before the Lord.

## Action Step

Psalm 56:8 tells us that God keeps a count of our tossings and puts our tears in a bottle. Affirming God's concern for you, give yourself permission to fall to pieces at His feet.

## Prayer

God, I can't hold this in any longer. I am laying all my shattered and broken pieces at Your feet. I will wait in Your presence as You heal and restore the barren places. Amen.

# Racing to Idle

*For you yourselves know how you ought to imitate us,*
*because we were not idle when we were with you.*
2 THESSALONIANS 3:7

*"Ladies, start your engines!"* This is the daily mantra I hear speeding through my mind as I strap in to find my way to the coveted place in line to do one thing . . . sit . . . engine running idle, waiting for movement to find its way to us. Winter afternoons implore you to keep the car on for needed heat to keep frostbite from taking your fingers and toes. Summer days long for the cool air to blow your hair in the wind.

From the afternoon car line to the after-school sports activities, sitting in this idle place is priority. You might find yourself here for a few minutes to an hour.

Even though this might be prime real estate for picking up and dropping off our children, Paul reminds us of the importance of not being idle in our life lived here on earth. Burning fuel, not going anywhere, is not what God had in mind.

Paul wrote this letter to the Thessalonian believers, reminding them of the work God had called them to, until Jesus returned. He implored them to follow his example so they would know how to live their lives. He went on to encourage them in verse 13 to not grow weary in doing good.

He got it. He knew the struggles they faced and that you and I face today. Paul endured these same difficulties and others we could not fathom. He stayed disciplined in the calling God placed on his life.

Have you found yourself sitting idle, knowing God is reminding you to put it in drive? He is ready to put fuel in your tank to help you get back to the work instilled in you to do.

## Action Step

Identify one place you have found yourself sitting idle. Seek the Lord in the first step to take, and go for it!

## Prayer

God, I am ready to get back to work! Thank You for refueling my life and giving me the gentle correction I need to move forward. Amen.

# Jesus Gets the Overwhelm

*And he took with him Peter and James and John, and began to be greatly distressed and troubled. And he said to them, "My soul is very sorrowful, even to death. Remain here and watch."*
MARK 14:33–34

Jesus knew what was about to happen. He knew the separation coming from His Father, something He had never experienced. Our Lord knew pain, judgment, and the weight of all sin that was about to land upon His shoulders.

He experienced overwhelming emotions, feelings, and situations. He has been where you have been. We know He was without sin, so what was His response?

First, we see Jesus being honest with friends. He did not hide what was going on inside and say, "I'm fine!" Jesus expressed it openly and without shame. Who are those comrades in your life with whom you can share the overwhelming feelings of your soul, knowing judgment will not be cast upon you?

We see our Lord pray to His Father with this same voice of sincerity and humility. Later in this passage, He cried out to God and called Him *Abba*, which is another way of saying Daddy. Christ was close to His Father and chose not to pretend. We are safe to lament to our good Father.

After Jesus finished praying, we see Him move forward in obedience to God's plan. He trusted His Father. Jesus didn't try to concoct a new plan or go His own way. Jesus knew salvation and redemption awaited us through His death and resurrection.

So, when the overwhelming comes, remember to follow the example of Christ: Talk to your trusted friends openly. Share with your heavenly Father honestly. Walk the way of the Father obediently.

## Action Step

Jesus gets your overwhelm. Pick one step He gave us to deal with the deluge of emotions and sorrow working overtime to halt you from walking in God's plan.

## Prayer

Abba, I need You. I am laying all of my overwhelm in Your hands. Help me to trust and walk in Your way. Amen.

# This Car Line Is Scary!

*For we walk by faith, not by sight.*
2 CORINTHIANS 5:7

A tiny, crackling voice came from the backseat as vehicles moved speedily in all directions. "This car line is scarwee!" my toddler shouted. Many were paying more attention to the buzzing of their phones, myself included, while horns blared, voices screamed out windows, and the adrenaline was pumping heavily through the air.

So many scary things were going on around us, but we had to stay focused and move toward our destination.

Our path here on this earth can be filled with the same terror my youngest felt that day. Darts are flying around like cars in the afternoon. You know God is calling you forward, but your flesh wants to honk the horn and put on the brakes.

Moving in faith doesn't require giant leaps. It may look like the sliding of a toe forward, then a baby step, to bounding a hurdle, to a marathon runner's pace. Faith is a process that advances much like our car lines every day. We won't always know who or what is surrounding us, but if we keep our eyes on the finish line, we will arrive.

How do we do it? How do we walk by faith even when we can't see where we are going?

When you wake up every morning, ask the Holy Spirit to give you courage as you aim your feet on the path you have been given. Take your gaze off what is intimidating you, and focus your mind on the one, true voice. Don't stop moving. Walking is an action that doesn't require ten steps ahead to be done—it just needs a solid place for each foot to land. God is already providing the next piece of concrete as your foot is in the air.

## Action Step

Go for a walk. Say today's verse out loud
as you move your feet forward.

## Prayer

Dear Lord, help me to no longer look at the darts flying
around me, but instead to aim my focus and trust
on You as I move my feet forward. Amen.

# Building a Home

*Unless the LORD builds the house, those who build
it labor in vain. Unless the LORD watches over the city,
the watchman stays awake in vain.*
PSALM 127:1

Have you found yourself in a place where you work, work, work, but nothing feels accomplished? Do you wake up exhausted as you try to get your household up and moving in the mornings and come home even more drained than when the day began? Do you wonder if doing more is causing you to achieve less?

I think if we were gathered around a living room space, all the moms would sing in unison, "Yes!"

In our never-ending efforts to create a home, the constant labor is done in vain. It is easy for us to "get to the work," before asking God if it is the job He would have us do. Often, good tasks will come our way and we assume it is from the Lord because it is good. We overlook the step of yielding and submitting to Him in prayer to ask if it is a God thing or just a good thing.

Take some time today and *stop*. Pray and ask the Lord if the house you are building is becoming the home He intended you to have. Submit your ways under His authority. Surrender all the hard work, plans, and goals you have into the most trusted hands. He will open your eyes to the exact building plan needed to create your home.

## Action Step 🏠

Write down all the work you do. Ask God if there is anything you need to remove or add.

## Prayer

Thank You, Lord, for being a Master Builder. Craft our home in Your best plan. Amen.

# Will You Help Me Carry This?

*But Moses' hands grew weary, so they took a stone and put it under him, and he sat on it, while Aaron and Hur held up his hands, one on one side, and the other on the other side. So his hands were steady until the going down of the sun. And Joshua overwhelmed Amalek and his people with the sword.*
EXODUS 17:12–13

It had to be the largest. There was no sneaking my way around this one. She wanted it to be the biggest, most orange, spectacular pumpkin we could find the night before the project was due. Her big, blue eyes lasered in on what she was looking for right when the grocery store doors opened.

We sat at the table that night creating a unicorn pumpkin. I will not divulge how much glitter was involved in case my husband is reading this and wondering where all the glitter is coming from several years later.

The next day, it was time to present her masterpiece to the classroom. She grabbed the pumpkin, and her eyes were as round as what she was holding. She realized the weight was too much to carry on her own.

"Will you help me carry this instead of driving through the car line?" Without hesitation, I made my way to carry what felt light in my hands.

Joshua was in a battle. Without Moses holding his hands up and interceding on his behalf, it was a lost cause. Moses grew tired trying to do it alone. Hur and Aaron jumped in to help carry the load. They crafted a plan together, allowing victory to be experienced by everyone.

What weight are you trying to carry that is too heavy? Who are your Aaron and Hur? What friends can you ask, "Will you help me carry this?"

## Action Step

Stop carrying the weight on your own.
Invite your Aaron and Hur to help you.

## Prayer

Dear heavenly Father, I needed this reminder
to not do life alone. Help me have courage to allow
my arm-bearers to hold the weight. Amen.

# Wash Me

*Have mercy on me, O God, according to your
steadfast love; according to your abundant
mercy blot out my transgressions. Wash me thoroughly
from my iniquity, and cleanse me from my sin!*
PSALM 51:1–2

As I ran to my car to get into the afternoon car line, I was brought to a screeching halt when I saw it . . . two words: *WASH ME!*

Kids have no mercy in making the grime caked on your car into a glorious work of art. I can just imagine the belly laughs filling my garage as little fingers painted in the pollen. There was no hiding or avoiding how dirty my car was now. It was evident it needed to be made clean.

David was fully aware of the transgressions in his heart. He saw the build-up and knew God's mercy was the only thing that could fully wash him and make him new inside.

We don't like to talk about our sin, the things we do, say, or think, that are not glorifying to God; but we need to be honest and realize that we do sin. We do make mistakes. Just as David took time to acknowledge where he had fallen short, we need to do the same.

Because God's love is steadfast, it is dedicated to blotting out our transgressions. His goodness cleanses us and makes us whole. When we go through this washing process, God creates a new heart within us. He gives us the deluxe wash, and it costs us nothing.

## Action Step

Confession time. Slow down in this moment, and ask God for forgiveness for any transgression you have been holding.

## Prayer

Dear God, forgive me for (fill in the blank). Have mercy on me, and blot out these transgressions from my life. Thank You for Your steadfast love and making me new. Amen.

# No More Should-ing on Yourself

*"For God did not send his Son into the world to condemn the world, but in order that the world might be saved through him."*
JOHN 3:17

> *"You should be on time for morning drop-off and not stress out your kids."*
>
> *"You should be as good a mom as your social media friends."*
>
> *"You should stop getting fast food for your family and get your act together with a home-cooked meal every night."*
>
> *"You should not have a laundry mountain that is unending, growing, day after day."*

Do any of these bully statements sound familiar? Have you heard yourself think these thoughts when you see your reflection in the mirror? We have to stop *should-ing* on ourselves. If God does not condemn us, we can call off the attack dogs we sic on ourselves.

How do we silence the "should" bully?

We remember that Jesus was sent here on a rescue mission. He was not sent here to condemn. Allow this love and forgiveness He freely gives to penetrate your heart. Confess Him as Savior and Lord of your life if you have not done this.

Dig into Scripture and what your heavenly Father is wanting to reveal to you of how He sees you. Some places to start:

> *Romans 6:6 (no longer a slave to sin)*
> *Romans 15:7 (you have been accepted by Christ)*
> *Romans 3:24 (you are justified and redeemed)*

Believe what God says—not just for others, but for yourself. God has not changed, which means He has not changed His mind about you. It has been the same since the beginning. Out of love He sent His one and only Son for you. He has lavished His love on you, and He is nearby to help you fight the bully thoughts with His truth!

## Action Step

Stop the whisper of the "should" bully.
Pick one of the Scriptures referenced above
and say it out loud every time a "should" attacks.

## Prayer

Dear Jesus, thank You for coming on a rescue mission for me.
You are the Savior and Lord of my life, and I choose to believe
what You say about me. Amen.

# It's Not Minuscule to God

*And whatever you do, in word or deed,*
*do everything in the name of the Lord Jesus,*
*giving thanks to God the Father through him.*
COLOSSIANS 3:17

It does matter. It is making a difference. What seems insignificant to you is substantial in the eyes of God.

You are walking out your role as a mom in the lives of a young generation all around you. When the eyes roll, they catch a seed of truth that plants in their soul. When the football cleats are left in the middle of the floor, again, the muttering prayers under your breath are being heard by your Good Father for their future. When you sit a little longer in the garage listening to stories of recess excitement and lunchroom drama, you are becoming a safe place for these tiny humans entrusted into your care.

Our verse reminds us that everything we do is done unto the Lord. Your day-to-day service does matter and is making an impact. As you move through these little things, ask the Lord to help you see them the way He does.

## Action Step

Go into the little things today with the truth
that you are making a big impact.

## Prayer

Dear God, I am grateful for this role You have given me. I know You see the little things making a considerable difference. Help me to see with this same vision. Amen.

# Crumbs in the Crevices

> *So that Christ may dwell in your hearts through
> faith—that you, being rooted and grounded in love,
> may have strength to comprehend with all the saints
> what is the breadth and length and height and depth,
> and to know the love of Christ that surpasses knowledge,
> that you may be filled with all the fullness of God.*
> EPHESIANS 3:17–19

Is it just me, or does your car accumulate wrappers of all colors? How about sticky suckers that were given up on and relinquished to the tiny holders in the door? Better yet, do you hear the crunching of crumbs beneath shoes or reach your hand down into the hole to grab your phone, and instead pull out a three-day-old French fry?

It is amazing what can seep into the teeniest crevice!

God's love for you and me works in this way too. He seems to find the places of hidden hurt and pours in-depth healing and restoration. He pulls back insecurity and replaces it with unconditional love. God doesn't miss one place of our being with His own.

Christ wants us to know the love He has for us. It's not afraid of the abyss of demeaning thoughts we have about ourselves nor is it held back by the trail mix of emotions our body feeds off of. This perfect affection He freely gives wipes out the enemy's scheme of hate.

When was the last time you allowed yourself to wrap up in your Daddy God's love? When was the last time you let your spirit be hugged by His goodness? When was the last time you granted yourself permission to dwell in this agape kind of love?

Jesus gives us this never-ending love, knowing we don't deserve it but desperately wanting us to receive it any way.

## Action Step

Stop running from this love you say you don't deserve. God knows this and yet graciously gives us this eternal gift.

## Prayer

Dear Jesus, I can't comprehend how or why You love me the way You do. Thank You for taking my place on the cross. Thank You for loving me with a love I don't deserve. Thank You for filling me with Your goodness. Amen.

# Are My Kids an Idol?

*And Samuel said to all the house of Israel, "If you are returning to the LORD with all your heart, then put away the foreign gods and the Ashtaroth from among you and direct your heart to the LORD and serve him only, and he will deliver you out of the hand of the Philistines."*
1 SAMUEL 7:3

Are your kids an idol?

I know that question probably feels totally in your face as you turn this page. We go from cracker crumbs together, to a question that causes us to scoff and then maybe ponder and then . . . conviction? It can be easy for us to wrap ourselves in our children's lives. What seems innocent at first begins to take a place of priority it was never meant to have. Yes, our children are important, but are they supposed to be our highest priority?

Israel made idols to Baal and Ashtaroth, and Samuel got their attention. They were lamenting to return to the Lord, but they needed to remove these false gods that had taken the place of the One True God. The Israelites followed Samuel's instructions and removed these golden images. They shifted their gaze back to where it belonged. By getting their lives back in alignment, God did bring victory over the Philistines.

Going back to the initial question, are our children an idol, what do we do if the answer is yes? First, confess and ask the Lord for forgiveness. Next, follow the example of the Israelites. Return your heart to God, and seek to glorify Him. Remove tendencies and habits that have caused you to put your children in a place they were never intended to be.

Our lives are not meant to revolve around our children. Setting this example for them will give the guidance they need in how to set godly priorities.

## Action Step

Make an honest list of your priorities. If things are out of order, take time with the Lord to get back in alignment with Him.

## Prayer

Heavenly Father, forgive me for allowing anything
to take precedence over You. I want You to be
the main priority in my life. Amen.

# Wait

*Wait for the LORD; be strong, and let your heart
take courage; wait for the LORD!*
PSALM 27:14

The line is moving, and then all of a sudden, the hand comes up for you to stop. So close! Just one more car and you would have been in that line to grab your youngling and off to wherever your next destination would be. We have all experienced this unwanted halt. I find myself either giggling or beating the steering wheel because I don't want to wait. I don't want to sit any longer.

I want to move.

I forget that waiting is an action. Waiting is needed. Waiting is important. Waiting can offer protection and a better spot. Waiting in God's presence delivers a refreshment to the soul. It's a cool drink from a glass of lemonade in the summertime.

There are days that will require the action of waiting. Being quiet and still before Him. Don't rush. Those few moments won't make you late, but they may make you different. As you linger, change is happening in His presence.

He is calling you in a little closer. He wants you to wait, remain with Him as He strengthens you and gives you courage. He sees the battles you are facing and knows the exhaustion you feel. His hand of pause is not a barricade, but an invitation to revive your spirit.

## Action Step 🌮

Wait. Wait a few extra moments in prayer
and silence as the Lord rejuvenates you.

## Prayer

Dear God, I want to sit at Your feet a few extra moments
today. Strengthen me with Your presence. Amen.

# Will the Insanity Ever End?

*Rejoice always.*
1 THESSALONIANS 5:16

Long days, crazy car lines, and insane schedules. The number of spinning plates above your head is growing by the second, and the ones that have fallen hit the ground like cymbals clanging at the end of a drum solo. The craziness seems to follow you in your dreams, and sleep becomes a scarcity in your life.

Do you ever find yourself asking when the madness will stop? Does this cycle of frenzy cause panic and worry to bring about an unwanted response from inside? Is the act of rejoicing something you think about doing in the midst of your circumstances, or does the thought of it cause a nervous laugh in your heart?

How do we rejoice when everything around us is turned upside down?

Paul wrote the answer to encourage the Thessalonians. Before arriving to chapter 5 in this letter, we find out in chapter 3 that he had received information from Timothy that warranted a firm but encouraging word. Paul knew they were being persecuted and wanted to give direction in how to respond. Paul goes on to emphatically declare for these believers to rejoice, not only when circumstances are easy, but *always*.

When it's painful, rejoice.

When it's scary, rejoice.

When it's hard, rejoice.

Rejoice . . . always rejoice.

The circumstances they endured did not stop joy from springing forth because the difficult situations did not change God.

Two simple words with powerful reverberation are still echoing to us today. Rejoice always. I don't know when the insanity will end, but I do know we can glorify the One who is walking through the shattered pieces of porcelain with us. He doesn't flinch in the midst of chaos, but offers us a steady hand as we delight in who He is.

## Action Step

No matter what circumstance comes your way today, rejoice.

## Prayer

God, I rejoice in *You*! You are worthy
of praise no matter what. Amen.

DAY 34

# But, What If . . .

*Finally, brothers, whatever is true, whatever is honorable,
whatever is just, whatever is pure, whatever is lovely, whatever
is commendable, if there is any excellence, if there is anything
worthy of praise, think about these things.*
PHILIPPIANS 4:8

Have you ever thought about the thoughts you think about
every day? They file in one right after the other. According to
the research of one well-respected brain clinic, we can have
up to 70,000 thoughts in twenty-four-hour period.[1] Some days
there are more, and others, there are less, but many of the
thoughts that bombard us are negative and on repeat. These
pessimistic views tend to come through the lens of fear and
worry. As moms, What IFs plague us:

- What IF I am failing my children?
- What IF I am failing my husband?
- What IF I am failing God?
- What IF something bad happens?
- What IF my kid is being bullied?
- What IF my kid *is* the bully?
- What IF . . . ?

1. https://healthybrains.org/brain-facts/

Our brain needs us to take charge of what gets to stay and where our focus will remain. We need to clear out the weeds of What IFs by retraining our thoughts to go to What IS.

Our Scripture gives us eight things to make an about-face with our thinking patterns. We can intentionally move our What IFs to What IS by spotlighting these truths in our mind.

What IS true:

- God is holy.
- God is in control.
- God has never failed us.
- God loves our children more than we do and He is with them.
- God knows everything about us and called us into the role we have been given.
- God is worthy of our praise no matter what the What IFs say.

## Action Step

Practice changing a What IF thought by using What IS. Write down or say out loud What IS true as you learn a new way of thinking.

## Prayer

Heavenly Father, help me to be intentional about what thoughts I allow to stay. Guide me in standing on What IS true no matter what the What IFs try to say. Amen.

# A Praying Mama

*For this reason I bow my knees before the Father.*
EPHESIANS 3:14

Waking up in the middle of the night thinking of our children, we wonder what will happen to them. What will they become? Are they dealing with mental struggles? Do they have battles at school that we know nothing about?

Tears flow, knees hit the carpet, and prayers commence.

Yelling matches echo at the kitchen sink before leaving for school. Doors slam as a punishment is given after a disobedient action. Can the tween's eyes possibly roll any farther back into their head?

Screams release, knees buckle, and prayers commence.

A broken heart from a devastating situation has filled your son's life. No answers and only arms to console the questions in your daughter's mind as an unthinkable situation with a friend occurs.

Silence halts your words, knees bend beside their bed, and prayers commence.

God uses a praying mama. He used mine. I still remember her sitting at the kitchen table as we got up every day for school. Her Bible open-wide with prayers for each of us. She still prays today.

Don't stop praying for your children. The Lord is listening.

Car Line MOM

## Action Step

Commence praying for your kids.

## Prayer

God, thank You for these children. Guide their feet
on the path You have for them. Amen.

# So Hard Letting Go

*Those who look to him are radiant,*
*and their faces shall never be ashamed.*
PSALM 34:5

Moms all across the world eventually come to terms with letting their kids go. It hits at certain points for each of us. We move from this place of celebrating every month and milestone with a sticker on the onesie, to a time when they make new discoveries without us. A spark of light comes bursting out when they land their first cartwheel in recess or catch a touchdown pass to win the game before PE ends.

It's hard to let go because we want to hold them close. We do it knowing growth is taking place in their heart and soul. Instead of leaning on us, they begin to experience God's goodness, faithfulness, and so much more. If we were to never let go and let them have these landmark moments, they would miss so much.

If we are honest, there is something else that is difficult for us to release. We hold it tight in the secret place of our heart. Instead of it being something that holds our children back, it is holding *us* back. We treat it like an old friend who is bad for us but has been faithful to remain over the years.

Shame.

We hold on to the shame of our past or the shame of moments from just this morning. We take a picture of it and enshrine it with a caption that pops back up in our memories year after year.

If God doesn't hold shame against us, it's time for us to say goodbye to this nagging companion. It is not our friend. Shame oppresses and stops us from turning our face to the compassionate glow of our Father.

Look to Him. Release the scandal you have held yourself under all this time. God's goodness and faithfulness will pierce the gray out of your soul, and your face will radiate His hope.

## Action Step

Write down the shame you have been holding. Physically throw it away as you throw it at the feet of Jesus.

## Prayer

God, thank You for not holding my past and my sins against me. Thank You for forgiveness. Amen.

# I Need Help

*Bear one another's burdens,*
*and so fulfill the law of Christ.*
GALATIANS 6:2

I used to think I had to have it all together and that if other moms knew the truth about me, they would reject me. I convinced myself that the mask of perfection was more important than being honest about the hardships I was facing. The weight of the world was silently crushing me from the inside out.

*Please, help me.*

Why are these words so hard to say? Very few of us willingly ask for help. We have convinced ourselves we need to figure everything out on our own. This life-saving action has earned a negative connotation over time. It isn't bad or a four-letter word, but this is how it gets treated.

When I finally began to reach out for help, things changed for the good. It wasn't easy, but over time it has become a new way of living.

Admitting we need help is a freeing feeling. God knew we would need one another to help with the strains of life. We can take off our mask and realize none of us have it all together.

Putting yourself in a place of isolation is dangerous. The weight of the mask you are wearing is not worth what you are going through. Your heavenly Father never intended for you to hide away. He is not mad at you for needing help. By reaching out for assistance, you are being obedient to what His Word tells us to do.

Your helpers might be a close friend or relative who will listen over coffee. It may look like reaching out to a counselor or doctor. Praying with your pastor or small group leader could be the step you need to take. However you feel led, surrender your mask and ask for help.

## *Action Step*

Ask for help. You no longer have to do it all alone.

## *Prayer*

Dear God, give me courage to ask for help. Amen.

# Mom, You Don't Understand!

*"For my thoughts are not your thoughts, neither are your ways my ways, declares the LORD. For as the heavens are higher than the earth, so are my ways higher than your ways and my thoughts than your thoughts."*

ISAIAH 55:8–9

Have you ever pulled the mom card and said, "I know you think I don't understand, but this is for your own good"? I have lost track of the number of times this statement has traveled out of my mouth and created disappointed faces. It takes me back to memories of being a teenager feeling the same blow of defeat when my parents didn't understand. Or so I thought.

As moms, we see from a place with a broader view than our kids. This gives us a better perspective on everything going on around them. When they ask for a social media app and we know the damage it can cause, the "no" is not to hurt them. It's a move of protection even though they don't understand. Or, if they ask you for a brownie right before bedtime and you give them a "no" wrapped in a hug because you know sugar makes their body party all night, it's for their benefit. We do what is best for them.

God operates in this same way for us. There are times He tells us no. We get upset and go back to Him explaining why it is a good idea, or how it won't hurt us like it may have caused pain for others. His gentle arm wraps around us to tell us, "I know you don't understand, but this is for your own good. My way is better for you." His vantage point is much higher than we can comprehend. God will always do what is best for His kids.

## Action Step

Write down one way God is moving in your life
you don't understand but you know is best.

## Prayer

God, thank You for leading me the best way I need to go. I choose to trust You even when I don't understand. Amen.

# Are We Going to Make It?

*And let us not grow weary of doing good, for in due*
*season we will reap, if we do not give up.*
GALATIANS 6:9

Hey mama . . . deep breath. It won't always look like this. The days of cold coffee, stale bagels, and crumpled homework on your floorboard won't last forever. The work you are doing right now on behalf of your children may not come to fruition for a few more years.

A plot of land not far from where I live is filled with different crops and vegetables every season. You will see the man who owns it from time to time pulling weeds, tilling the ground, or using his tractor to prepare a new section. This process is important to make sure the harvest comes to completion. The work is hard, but every step counts. If he were to throw his hands up and quit too soon, he would miss out on his reward.

Don't give up. You are digging through some hard pieces of ground right now. The good soil you are getting to will be ripe, ready to be planted. Speaking God's Word over them will allow the seeds to sprout strong roots. Continue to pour water over their souls through the tears you shed during long nights of prayer. Teach them how to put up scarecrows of protection when the enemy wants to come in and plunder what God is doing in their life.

After all of this, a season is coming when you will obtain your reward. I can't lay out God's exact timing or specific plan for you, but I can confidently say He is bound to His Word. Your harvest may look like grandchildren being raised in church. It could be your children gathered around your table serving you a hot cup of coffee with a fresh cream cheese-filled bagel.

In the end, none of those things are the true reward. The eternal, never-ending benefit will be when you hear, *"Well done"* from your heavenly Father himself, no matter how your kids' lives shake out.

## Action Step

Write a letter to your future self when the kids are grown and out of the house. Use that letter to be an encouragement you can look to when you feel like giving up.

## Prayer

Heavenly Father, thank You for the reminder that this is only a season, but an important one. Give me strength to not give up and to keep tilling the ground for the harvest to come. Amen.

# Detour

*The heart of man plans his way,*
*but the LORD establishes his steps.*
PROVERBS 16:9

*DETOUR* is the last sign you want to see as you drive your kids to school. We put ourselves on specific schedules to leave at a certain time to get to each location. When unexpected things come up redirecting the route, it can cause a frenzy to stir in your heart and in the backseat.

Two days in a row we experienced the dreadful *DETOUR*. The deviation from our normal path caused me to blow steam out of frustration. My teenager chuckled and said, "Mom, it's no big deal. We will still get to where we are going, just in a different way." She was right.

How often do we get disheartened when God throws a *DETOUR* in our life?

It can be easy to find ourselves trying to play the role of God and telling Him which path we are going to take, the stops we are going to make, and all that is at stake if it doesn't go the way we command. When our flesh moves us into this pattern of living, it's time to take a step back.

The Lord did not intend for us to say, "Here's the plan for *You* to follow." Rather, He would have us ask, "What is

*Your* plan, Lord? Where would You have my foot to step?" Submitting our desires and agendas will bring glory to God.

When the *DETOURS* come, remember He has a purpose behind them. Release the fear and worry, and trust He knows where you are going. What you will discover is the *DETOUR* is much better than your original course of direction.

## Action Step

The next time you have a *DETOUR*, pray and ask the Lord if He is wanting to reveal a change needed in your life.

## Prayer

God, where would You have my foot step today?
I submit my plans and desires to Your will. Amen.

# The Newbie

*As each has received a gift, use it to serve one another,*
*as good stewards of God's varied grace.*
1 PETER 4:10

Heart racing. Palms sweating. Breath rapidly gaining speed. I can still recall this feeling as I entered afternoon pick-up for the very first time. I was the newbie who found herself in the wrong line. I was *that* one. Everything went downhill from there.

Do you remember being the new mom? New to car line? New to drop-off? Feeling overwhelmed, sensing the death stares from all the other cars around you? There are other newbies going through this even as you read. They are belittling themselves for making mistakes. They are embarrassed by the car jams they caused by arriving five minutes too early. These newbies to the car line are turning all shades of red as they realize they have been waiting in the wrong section for thirty minutes, and they arrived with such great confidence.

How can you use your gift as an experienced car line mom to encourage the newbies around you?

Think back to what would have been helpful when you first started stopping and going in and out of these new lanes. Reach out to these first-timers and let them know we all make mistakes in the beginning. Share your battle stories to add normalcy to the deluge of emotions they are experiencing.

Give them practical tips to put into place such as practicing the route they need to take to physically lay their eyes on the lane they will be in.

Ultimately, let the new moms know you are praying for them and are there to help however you can. Offering your gift of experience will shine the light of God's grace into a heart that needs to know she isn't alone.

## Action Step

Reach out to a newbie mom. Ask her how she
is doing and what is most overwhelming to her.
Encourage and pray for her.

## Prayer

Dear Lord, show me the newbie moms You have
put in my path to encourage and lift up. Help me
to shine Your love into their life. Amen.

# No Time for Quiet Time

*The steadfast love of the LORD never ceases;*
*his mercies never come to an end; they are new*
*every morning; great is your faithfulness.*
LAMENTATIONS 3:22–23

Multiple alarms were set. My clothes were out with the cutest pair of shoes. Clean sheets awaited me as my plan to get up early was put into motion. Just one problem . . . nothing went as planned. As I reached up to snooze the alarms, I turned them all off. Panic shook me awake as I realized I had just enough time to get my kids up, lunches packed, and backpacks thrown into the car to make it before the bell rang. Unfortunately, the stylish shoes did not match my flannel pajama pants, so they remained on the floor as I whisked us all away.

Have you ever experienced this type of morning? I wish I could say this has only happened once, but in full transparency, there have been numerous times when the late start caused me to not include time alone with the Lord.

When things don't go as scheduled, we can remember His mercies are new every morning. He doesn't give us leftover grace or crumbs of His love. He gives it fully, not based on what we do, but on who He is.

The next time your view of daylight comes later than you anticipated, don't allow apprehension to take you to a place where you dread how the rest of the day is going to go. Instead, talk to the Lord while you are in the shower. Take five minutes to read through Scripture that has impacted your life. Allow His mercy to wash over you and cling to the gift of grace. Pivot your agenda so time with God takes place. It's okay if it doesn't look the way you planned.

## Action Step

Break the habit of hitting snooze, and get up as soon as the alarm goes off tomorrow! Try having water on your bedside table to help you get up and get moving.

## Prayer

Dear Lord, I am grateful for Your never-ending mercy and grace. Amen.

# Buckle Up

*Stand therefore, having fastened
on the belt of truth.*
EPHESIANS 6:14A

"Buckle up!" This command rings daily out of every vehicle. Moms everywhere are reminding the little ones placed in their care to fasten their seat belts. We do this as a form of protection for sudden stops, for increases in speed, and against possible danger around us. If we do not use it, a mishap could happen that could have been prevented.

This safety strap does us no good if it is not put into action.

Paul goes to great lengths to shed light on the spiritual battles we will face and how important it is to put on the armor of God to stand against Satan. The assault against us is not one created by human hands, so it requires a spiritual defense we must put into motion regularly.

The belt of truth is the first piece of armor we are told to put on. It is closest to the body. We know our adversary will throw darts of lies to penetrate our souls. The truth of the gospel pushes back and reveals this deception. Fastening truth around our waist will cause us to walk in integrity and noble character. When this belt is buckled, it secures the breastplate of righteousness. We can then put on our shoes of peace, hold our shield of faith, place our helmet of salvation on our heads, and grip the sword of the Spirit as we stand firm against our attacker.

## Action Step

Put truth on every day. If a falsehood slips through, test it against Scripture so that it doesn't loosen the belt.

## Prayer

Heavenly Father, You have given me this armor to use every day. Help me to buckle up and be ready to stand against the attacks of my enemy. Amen.

# First, Wash Your Hands!

*"But seek first the kingdom of God and his righteousness,*
*and all these things will be added to you."*
MATTHEW 6:33

Before a cookie can touch their lips, a finger can swipe up, or a bike leaves the garage, first things first when we get home from school or afternoon activities. Hands must be washed and sanitized from all the germs that have gleefully gathered throughout the day. These tiny organisms love a basketball and baton!

Washing off the dirt leads to enjoying better things. The longer it takes to complete this simple task, the less fun my kids get to enjoy.

We miss out on savoring this life when we don't do first things first. Our focus shifts to what we need to accomplish to make things happen and have our needs met. Stress creeps in, activating unnecessary worry. Our thoughts plummet us days and months into a future brimming with worst-case scenarios that will never happen but emerge in a realistic vision. Our knees drop in prayer, begging God to not allow those schemes to play out.

How different would our lives look if we reversed this plot of action and started with where we end? By seeking the Lord first, it transforms everything. It prevents evil parasites from misguiding our steps. We stop placing unmerited pressure on our shoulders trying to play God's role in our lives. We move from angst to peace, knowing He will supply every need. Our thinking will look to a future with Him guiding every situation.

## Action Step

Every time you wash your hands, remind yourself to seek the Lord first and not last. He has everything you need.

## Prayer

Thank You, Lord, for meeting all my needs. You never withhold any good thing from me. Amen.

# Windows Down

*For freedom Christ has set us free; stand firm therefore,*
*and do not submit again to a yoke of slavery.*
GALATIANS 5:1

There are mornings Cooper Hashbrown gets to enjoy the ride to school. His fluffy, brown fur blows in the wind as he sits up tall in the passenger seat. A bark or two may escape as his sisters exit, but when the car goes into drive, a doggy smile lands on his face. My youngest will bask in the afternoon warmth when the windows are down. The steady breeze blows through her hair, releasing extra chatter from the back of the car. When the sunroof is cracked, it adds a further element of freedom as we coast into the neighborhood.

When the windows are up, we are confined to only experiencing the limited air the car allows. When the windows are down, we partake in a boundless gust.

When Jesus came to this earth, He arrived on assignment to set captives free. He broke off the bondage of slavery through His death on the cross. Galatians 3:23–24 reminds us we are no longer under Mosaic Law but justified by faith because of Christ.

Living through faith rolls the windows down to experience the immeasurable love of God. It compels us to freely serve Him and others. We no longer feel handcuffed to a religious task list. Rather, we want to share this gift of grace with every-one around us.

## Action Step

How can you humbly serve others around you through the love of Christ to reveal the freedom He has for them?

## Prayer

Thank You, Jesus, for setting me free!

# Friend to Everyone

*Beloved, let us love one another, for love is from God, and whoever loves has been born of God and knows God.*
1 JOHN 4:7

As my daughters put their backpacks on and grab their lunches to glide out of the seat and onto the concrete, we recite reminders of how to live for the day. It is a monotonous list to them, but it is a beautiful melody to my ears. One of the essential principles is to be a friend to everyone and treat others the way they want to be treated.

Pretty simple but not always uncomplicated.

This straightforward way of living tends to leave all our minds at some point. As adults, it is a mindless thing to get caught up in our own inner conflict or busyness of the day. We overlook those who are not in our typical circle, or we assume the worst of someone if they speak to us in an agitated voice. Our flesh naturally leans to an unfavorable response.

It is time to make a change.

The guidelines we give our children are important commands God has placed on us. God bestowed love on us, so who are we to withhold love from others? If we were to pause in our thoughts of those we work with, sit next to on the bleachers, or stand behind in the coffee shop, we would be slower to cast judgment. The love of God would open our hearts to the fact that this may be a difficult season they are walking through. When we choose to be a friend and show kindness, we are shining the light of Jesus into their weary soul.

## *Action Step* 📖

Who can you be a friend to today? Write their name down, and pray for an opportunity to show kindness to them.

## *Prayer*

God, will You help me to have compassion for others the way You do? Allow love, instead of frustration, to come from my actions. Amen.

# Can You Pick Me Up First?

*"So the last will be first, and the first last."*
MATTHEW 20:16

Please tell me this epic battle of who will be first is not just happening behind *my* car doors. Most of our days are dictated by the activities of the afternoon allowing this argument to be silenced before it can begin. There are cycles of time when it could go either way. Both girls have solid explanations for why they should be first, but ultimately, someone has to be last.

I can relate to this clash with your sibling. I have a twin brother, and I am one minute older than him. As a kid, I would relish in the sixty seconds of being born first. Now that I am older, I would prefer to be the youngest.

It is in our nature to want to be first.

Thankfully, God doesn't operate according to our flesh. He doesn't do things the way the world would. His way of doing things appears backward to the world. Why on earth would someone put themselves last? Why would anyone look for ways to serve rather than be the one served?

This is how Jesus operates. He was always ready to give an encouraging word, feed hungry families, or wash the feet of those on the mission field. His example gives clarity to why we would desire to be last. By serving others, we are devoting ourselves to the way of living that God has called us to. No, we won't receive many earthly rewards for looking to be last. But we will store up treasure in heaven.

## Action Step

Identify one way you can put yourself
last and serve someone else.

## Prayer

Jesus, You gave me beautiful examples of how to love and
serve others. Help me to follow Your lead. Amen.

# She Is Not Your Competition

*Now there are varieties of gifts, but the same Spirit;*
*and there are varieties of service, but the same Lord;*
*and there are varieties of activities, but it is the*
*same God who empowers them all in everyone.*
1 CORINTHIANS 12:4–6

The woman with perfect hair and make-up in morning drop-off is not your enemy.

The mama who cooks a homemade dinner five times a week is not your enemy.

The female who posts daily inspiration on all her social media platforms is not your enemy.

The mom who makes it to every single ball game is not your enemy.

The lady who attends all PTO meetings is not your enemy.

The mom who always beats you to the best spot in afternoon car line is not your enemy.

Our *true* enemy is very clever to cause us to view one another as the antagonist in each of our stories. Satan wants us to doubt the skill set God gave us to use by comparing it to the mom waiting in line behind us. He twists our perception of inadequacies as a place we will never measure up next to her.

This is a lie from the "accuser of our brothers," as Revelation 12:10 calls him.

God *did* give each and every one of us different gifts and abilities on purpose. He created us diverse to work together as *one* body. We are all empowered by God to work together.

The variety of talents we have can ignite a revival within our communities when we begin to see each other as comrades in arms. Now when you see her, look at her as a fellow warrior. Lift her up in prayer when her name travels through your thoughts. Wave with a smile the next time you see her in line. As we make this shift in how we see each other, the ripple effects will be felt in car lines everywhere.

We are putting Satan on watch. He messed with the wrong group of women.

## Action Step

Write this statement down: She is not my enemy.

## Prayer

Dear God, thank You for the warrior mamas You have placed in my life. Bring our gifts together to reach our community for You! Amen.

# We Have a Garden at School!

*He makes me lie down in green pastures. He leads me
beside still waters. He restores my soul. He leads me
in paths of righteousness for his name's sake.*
PSALM 23:2–3

A Styrofoam cup greeted me one afternoon as my daughter jumped in the car. "We have a new garden at school!" This outdoor classroom created a unique experience for our kids to learn how to grow different types of vegetables. The tiny seedling cupped in her hands came with a responsibility to water and give it daily sunlight. The first few days we did great with the assignment. But missing one day of water caused our little plant to shrivel up. We couldn't revive this unknown vegetable. I think it was a tomato, but we will never know since we could not replenish it with the daily drink it needed.

Do you find yourself shriveling? Are you shrinking away from your source of life?

Get back into the herd. Move back under His staff. The Good Shepherd knows your soul needs daily refreshment just like my daughter's seed in a cup. He makes you lie down in green pastures to offer protection and life-giving sustenance. The calm water God can pour into you offers refreshment and rest. His supply is unending.

As you drink from His water source, rest will renew your production of fruit.

## *Action Step*

Rest in God's presence. Make yourself sit still or
lie down, and ask God to refresh your soul.

## *Prayer*

Lord, I'm tired. I need a drink from Your still waters. Renew my soul and help me to simply rest in Your presence. Amen.

# Hat Down, Sunglasses Up

*But he himself went a day's journey into the wilderness and
came and sat down under a broom tree. And he asked that he
might die, saying, "It is enough; now, O LORD, take away his
life, for I am no better than my fathers."*
1 KINGS 19:4

Hat down as far as it could go, and sunglasses on to block the
glare of the sun. Being seen was the last thing on my agenda,
so looking invisible made more sense. I went to a store not in
my local area to grab one item. A familiar voice came around
the corner. Eye contact was difficult to make, but I was able to
string together a sentence of small talk. A fake smile sent her
away unbeknownst to the reality I was hiding.

I had found myself in a place like Elijah. I wanted to die.
Fear consumed my every thought. Dread greeted me when I
opened the blinds. Closing them back seemed to silence the
doomsday voices for a moment. When I hit the bottom of this
dark hole, God was there with His compassionate hands tilting
my chin up to see hope.

Have you found yourself in this situation? Are you struggling in silence?

Just as God met Elijah in his depressive state and me in
mine, He will do the same for you. The Lord sent an angel to
Elijah in his distress and told him to eat and drink. He followed

these practical steps and then slept. When he got up, God sent Elijah back on his path and included a community around him.

Practical steps of feeding your body and removing an overdone schedule will allow your body to get back in order. Find a community of believers you can walk this path with as God brings healing and restoration into your life. Don't hesitate to reach out to a counselor to help you uproot any hindrance from your past keeping you from moving forward in the purpose God has for you.

## Action Step 🌅

Which practical step do you need to take? Are you physically hungry? Do you need to let community back into your life? Have you been pondering reaching out to a counselor? Pick one step to take.

## Prayer

God, I need a helping hand. I know You have a purpose for me, but unbelief is creeping in. Holy Spirit, speak truth to my heart as I begin to take practical steps to healing. Amen.

# You Must Circle and Start Again

*But Ruth said, "Do not urge me to leave you or to return from following you. For where you go I will go, and where you lodge I will lodge. Your people shall be my people, and your God my God."*

RUTH 1:16

The map gave clear instruction on the path we were to take. If we did not follow the procedure correctly, we had to circle the car line and start again. Entering wherever we desired and creating our own path was not an option. Following the guidance set in place brought humility, accountability, and order. It was painful to exit the car line and start again.

Ruth found herself in a place of humility, having to begin again. Her husband was dead. Naomi, her mother-in-law, was mourning the loss of her sons and husband. She implored Ruth to circle back and go home and not follow her to Bethlehem. Ruth resisted this request. She didn't want to start again without Naomi in her life. She was determined to follow Naomi and her God.

Ruth looked up to Naomi. She felt accountable to take care of her. Ruth found herself gleaning from the field of Boaz, a relative of Naomi. God moved on behalf of Ruth and Naomi. Her humble spirit and honorable character placed her in the lineage of David as his great-grandmother and an ancestor to Jesus.

Have you found yourself in a place of starting again? Who do you have in your life who can hold you accountable to walking in a way that is pleasing to the Lord?

God brought redemption to Ruth and Naomi in unexpected ways. Their fresh start was uncomfortable and required perseverance. Your circle around may include bumps in the road, but as you endure, the Lord will not forget you. The plan He has for you is too astonishing to show it all at once. Follow Him one turn at a time.

## Action Step

Who is one friend in your life you will reach out
to as an accountability partner?

## Prayer

Heavenly Father, as I circle around, I will trust You
through every bump, stop, and wait. I know Your
redeeming power is at work in my life. Amen.

# Boo!

*And he said to him, "Please, Lord, how can I save Israel?*
*Behold, my clan is the weakest in Manasseh, and I am the least*
*in my father's house." And the LORD said to him, "But I will be*
*with you, and you shall strike the Midianites as one man."*
JUDGES 6:15–16

My kids love to jump out and scare each other! Anyone else's? They know better than to scare me because it would not end well for anyone. My reactions can be dangerous.

Gideon was not one who liked to be scared. We find him beating wheat while hiding in a wine press. This young man was afraid of the circumstances going on around him. When the angel of the Lord found him, he identified Gideon as a mighty man of valor. As the messenger sent by God told Gideon the plan to strike down the Midianites, he responded with a rebuttal filled with reasons why he was not the right guy.

Have you ever done this? Have you ever given God a laundry list of items pointing out the reasons why you can't do what He is asking you to do? Has fear caused you to hide away the strength placed inside you?

God did not respond to Gideon in an angry tone. He gently let Gideon know, "I will be with you." Gideon was scared but walked in what God told him to do. He had a lot of questions and doubts but faced the situation head-on. Through

Gideon, three hundred men, trumpets, and empty jars, God brought victory!

What is fear yelling at you? No matter how loud the megaphone of fear, a whisper of faith will drown it out. God is with you!

## Action Step 🥡

It's time to come out of hiding. Write down what God is calling you to do, and take one step in the opposite direction fear is trying to move you.

## Prayer

Lord, I have lots of questions in this direction You are leading me. But I will go each step You lead. Thank You for grace in the questions I ask. Amen.

# No Car Line Today

*As a deer pants for flowing streams, so pants my*
*soul for you, O God. My soul thirsts for God, for the living God.*
*When shall I come and appear before God?*
PSALM 42:1–2

Pounding feet barreled into our bedroom at midnight. I willed myself to open one eye to discover which child was standing next to the bed. My oldest was clinging to her stomach ready to explode at any moment. I quickly scooted her away from my side of the bed and into the bathroom. Following from behind at a safe distance, I made sure she got over the toilet and not on my rug. I was zero help.

Many of you have the compassion trait. As you can see, I do not have the best bedside manner. My daughter had to hold her own hair and walk back to her bedroom with the throw-up bowl. The moral support I offered from ten feet away did not bring her the comfort she needed. Knowing she would not be going to school that day did give her some relief. Not having to go through two car lines helped me go back to sleep with ease.

What do we do when the core of our being is sick and needs care beyond human hands?

God is the only One who can repair the depths of our souls. Our Great Physician is where we turn. He will not stand far away from you while you crouch over in pain. The Lord will be the one to hold your hair back and wipe your tears. He won't send you back to your room alone with a bucket. Your heavenly Father will carry you until your soul is strong enough to stand again.

## Action Step

Run to your Great Physician. It will not be too messy for Him.

## Prayer

God, my core needs a healing touch from You. My soul longs for the living water only You can pour out. Amen.

# Tell Your Children

*That the next generation might know them,
the children yet unborn, and arise and tell them to their
children, so that they should set their hope in God and not
forget the works of God, but keep his commandments.*
PSALM 78:6–7

This young generation being raised up faces a major dilemma. Even though they are more connected than any other group, these young people are the most lonely. Desperately searching for real connection, all they can find are artificial likes and comments. It gives them a high for a moment but leaves their hearts empty inside.

This group longs to be accepted. The world gives them a guide to go by to be loved and approved, but the rules are constantly switching and the nonstop changes of what these teens must do to be "loved" is confusing. Instead of hearing this berating message of what they must do to be permitted in, these youths need to hear the truth that Jesus did all that needed to be done on the cross for them.

How do we get this message out to them?

Tell the ones in your care of God's goodness. Share personal testimonies of how the Lord has moved in your life. Sit down as a family to read Bible stories and talk through lessons to learn. Teach them the truth, and give them space to ask questions when they don't understand. Invite their friends into these conversations who may not have a home where the Bible is taught.

We are always one generation away from not knowing God and all He has done. If we don't tell them, who will?

## Action Step

Begin a family Bible reading time. We cannot let this generation grow up not knowing the goodness of God.

## Prayer

Lord, give us a heart of compassion for
this younger generation. They desperately desire
love and acceptance. You provide what they are searching for.
Give us boldness to share with them. Amen.

# Mom Crisis

*"Therefore do not be anxious, saying, 'What shall we eat?'
or 'What shall we drink?' or 'What shall we wear?' For the
Gentiles seek after all these things, and your heavenly Father
knows that you need them all."*
MATTHEW 6:31–32

It's hard to admit, but we cannot fix all the things for our kids. As much as we would like to be in multiple places at once solving all the problems and protecting their fragile hearts, we were not created to play that role. When we try to assume control that is not ours, the Mom Crisis Mode takes over, throwing us into a panicked frenzy.

What can we do when this catastrophe mode wants to take over, filling our body with anxious feelings? Stop and take three to four deep breaths. On every inhale and exhale remind yourself that YHWH is in control and not in crisis mode.

Write down the anxious thoughts, and take them captive. Rip them up, and throw them away, releasing their control. Replace them with the truth of God's Word by placing power-ful Scripture everywhere you need the reminders.

Pray a prayer of thanksgiving over your children and God's hand on their lives. Allow gratitude to block anxiety's power over you.

God chose you to be their mother. When your body attempts to throw you in Mom Crisis Mode, use one of these tactics to quickly bring you back to a place of calm.

No time for a crisis today.

## *Action Step*

Pick one of the practical steps given to implement today, and practice using it.

## *Prayer*

God, I acknowledge You are in control. I relinquish any grand idea thinking that I know better than You. Amen.

# Screechy Brakes Still Work

*And God is able to make all grace abound to you,*
*so that having all sufficiency in all things at all times,*
*you may abound in every good work.*
2 CORINTHIANS 9:8

*Screeeeech.*

I heard this noise as I pulled up to let my daughter out. We both looked at each other and then around trying to figure out where on earth the sound was coming from. I took my foot off the brake to move down a bit more, and we heard it again.

Me . . . it was me making that terrible noise. She and I shared a giggle and a glance as she walked in for another day of learning. I rolled my windows up and ducked down driving away. Even though it didn't sound great, the brakes still worked.

I have some good news! You are right . . . you are insufficient. You do not have it all together. You are weak and lack in certain areas. You are not enough on your own.

Before you throw the book out the window, give me a moment to explain why this is good news.

Acknowledging our frailty and fallenness takes the pressure off of trying to have it all together. We are imperfect beings in need of a perfect Savior. God knew we would need grace in an infinite amount to make it through each day.

This overflow of grace allows us to thrive in the good works God intends for each one of us to do. Let this gift wash over the insufficient places. You might squeak a little here and there, but His strength will carry you to the place you are intended to be.

## Action Step

Acknowledge your squeaky brakes, and take the pressure off.

## Prayer

God, You know my insufficient places. Pour Your grace out, and let Your strength overflow in the good works You have prepared for me. Amen.

# I Got a Boo-Boo

*Then he said to Thomas, "Put your finger here, and*
*see my hands; and put out your hand, and place it*
*in my side. Do not disbelieve, but believe."*
JOHN 20:27

The toddler years were filled with a never-ending supply of Band-aids around our home. Boo-boos came in large and small sizes. Sometimes, they were even invisible. No matter what appearance the scrape gave, the colorful bandage made everything better. But there were moments when the covering would be removed and a scar remained.

Scars and bruises. Jesus had them. He didn't hide them. When Jesus was resurrected out of the grave, He kept the scars in His hands, side, and feet. Jesus could have come back with no scars. I have always been curious as to why He kept them. It is pure speculation until we see Him face to face to ask.

I wonder if Jesus kept the scars knowing Thomas would need to see them. His love for the disciples and us is so deep and wide. He will connect with us even when we question and doubt.

His scars remind us He understands pain, ridicule, rejection, and being alone. All these things you and I have experienced, Jesus went through as well. We have a Savior who did not hide His scars, so we no longer have to hide our own.

The scars on Jesus tell the story of salvation. What do your scars tell? What testimony has God written in the markings on your life? Take the Band-aids off, and let His healing speak.

## Action Step

Write down your testimony. Take time to remember all the ways God has moved in your life.

## Prayer

Thank You, Jesus, for keeping Your scars and reminding me that You understand. Amen.

# Teaching the Young
# the Ways of Old

*Older women likewise are to be reverent in behavior,*
*not slanderers or slaves to much wine. They are to*
*teach what is good, and so train the young women*
*to love their husbands and children.*
TITUS 2:3–4

Every Sunday my husband and I look for her from the stage. This seasoned lady with beautiful silver hair sits in the front row and worships. She is unable to stand but sits and sings with all her might. Her hands move in rhythm to the worship song in her heart. Her legs may not be able to hold her up like they used to, but her heart is standing tall on who God is.

When we take time to look to those no longer in the car line, they can provide us with great wisdom and advice. They can give us guidance on what to embrace and what to erase. When we are in the midst of this hectic life, it is easy to get caught up in the weeds. Their perspective will be much broader now that they are on the other side of the line. Just as seasoning adds flavor and goodness to our food, it does the same in every area of our life.

We need mentors in our life much like Timothy had with Paul. He was able to encourage and challenge Timothy. Paul taught him the ways of old, allowing him to stand firm in difficult times.

Pray and ask the Lord to bring a mentor into your life if you do not yet have one. If you do, ask God to reveal a young mom to you who you can mentor.

## Action Step

Who is your mentor? Write down her name, and invite her to coffee as you ask her into this area of your life.

## Prayer

Dear heavenly Father, I need a Paul in my life. Reveal her to me, and help me to be a mentor to someone else. Amen.

# Time to Unpack the Lunch Box

*Let all bitterness and wrath and anger and clamor
and slander be put away from you, along with
all malice. Be kind to one another, tenderhearted,
forgiving one another, as God in Christ forgave you.*
EPHESIANS 4:31–32

The bell rings, summer begins, and backpacks disappear. I never see them again until the day before school starts as a new year is staring us in the face. I always forget to remove the lunch box before vacation. Let me rephrase: it escapes me to tell my kids to discard the turkey sandwiches, apple, and half-eaten brownie.

Do you know what happens when you open this mystery box in August? Some of you do and you feel the gagging sensation with me because it awaits you every year. There is a smell you cannot comprehend. The bread is green and yellow with a soft fuzz on top. The apple is squishy and bruised. Miraculously, the brownie appears safe, but you throw it out knowing nothing is as it appears to be.

Our souls can mimic these three-month-old leftovers. We have zipped up past hurts and secret embarrassment. If we were to open it, the stench of bitterness would throw us back into memories we are having a difficult time releasing.

It is time to unpack the lunchbox in your heart. The unforgiveness, anger, bitterness, and hurt you have been holding onto is causing pain to you, not those who instigated the dispute. Stop drinking the poison thinking it is burning them.

Let it go. Those three words are easier to read and type than to actually act upon. Your mental and physical health are worth it. Jesus gave us a forgiveness we did not deserve. As you forgive those who have wronged you, your action is following Christ. Forgiveness does not mean giving them free reign in your life.

Your act of forgiving is being obedient to the will of the Father. As you unpack and throw out all the stinky stuff, God renews you with a clean box. He even places a sweet letter on top to remind you of the love He has for you.

## Action Step

Write a goodbye letter to the bitterness and pain in your heart. Release forgiveness as you throw away the letter.

## Prayer

God, this bitterness is too stinky and painful. Help me to forgive those who caused this pain. Amen.

# I Can't Wait to Tell You about My Day!

*As he was getting into the boat, the man who had been possessed with demons begged [Jesus] that he might be with him. And he did not permit him but said to him, "Go home to your friends and tell them how much the Lord has done for you, and how he has had mercy on you."*

MARK 5:18–19

Some of the best days are when my kids get in the car and don't need to be prodded to share all the good news. They want to tell me about the best joke at the lunchroom table, or the good feeling about a test, talking with friends, and helping a teacher. They can't wait to tell me about their day.

What good things do you have to share with others in your circle who need to know of all God has done for you? The man in Scripture went on to do as Jesus commanded. He proclaimed God's goodness, and everyone marveled at the miracle performed in his life.

There are people all around you desperately needing to hear how God is still moving. He is not just a God of the past, but of the present. They need to know His Word is alive and so is He. Souls are longing to hear the testimonies and miracles that the Lord has done for you.

The enemy will do his best to silence you and tell you that if you testify you are bragging or rubbing it in someone's face. He does not want the people around you to know God continues to break out miracles and do the impossible. When this message gets out, faith comes alive and moves mountains.

## Action Step

What is something good God has done on your behalf? Share it with your friends through a text message or social media post. Give Him all the glory!

## Prayer

I praise You, God, for (fill in the blank). Thank You for working on my behalf! Amen.

# Uh-Oh . . .
# I Forgot My Kid!

*There is therefore now no condemnation
for those who are in Christ Jesus.*
ROMANS 8:1

The preschool director's number flashed across my screen. It was my husband's turn to pick up our daughter from school that day. I was a bit perplexed by why she was calling because school had been over for a good thirty minutes. Why would she need to call if my daughter was already gone for the day? Unless . . . she was still there!

You guessed it. My sweet husband had forgotten to go get her. She was safely stowed away on the playground with the other children still waiting to be picked up. After laughter filled the other side of the phone, I realized he was driving up as we were ending this unexpected conversation.

Anyone else ever experience forgetting a child? I would love to tell you grace and understanding poured out of my mouth as I called my husband to get the story. However, I was on the other end of the spectrum. A judging attitude and a condemning pointer finger are what I greeted him with when they arrived home.

Thankfully, God does not condemn us when we make a mistake or forget our children. Jesus was the blood atonement for our sins. When He died on the cross, condemnation died too. His sacrifice set us free from guilt. In our mom fails, we can confess, turn away from the sin and the shame, and run to God. The Lord forgives. And if He doesn't hold on to those failures, neither should you.

## Action Step

Stop shaming yourself over past mistakes.
It is for freedom that Christ has set you free.

## Prayer

Heavenly Father, if You do not condemn me, help me to stop shaming myself. Thank You, Jesus, for paying the price for my sin. Help me to walk in the freedom You have given me. Amen.

# Ma'am, Your Coffee
# Is on Top of Your Car

*He delivered us from such a deadly peril, and he will deliver us.*
*On him we have set our hope that he will deliver us again.*
2 CORINTHIANS 1:10

I could not believe my eyes. As I drove through the drop-off line, a traveling coffee cup was riding with ease on top of the car next to me. The shock muted my voice, but my daughter snapped me back into action with her snicker from the backseat. Waving my hands in the air did not get this lady's attention. Stopping the flow of traffic is never a good idea, but I noticed her window was down.

"Um, ma'am! Your coffee is on top of your car!"

I knew it sounded ridiculous as her look of confusion met my awkward smile. I pointed up and motioned my hand to my mouth pretending to drink a cup of coffee. When she arrived to a stopping point, she jumped out and grabbed the drink. A gesture of thanks came from her vehicle, and we were both on our way.

Even though this scenario ended with hot coffee delivered to her soul, it fails in comparison to the hope God delivers in our life over and over. He will always meet us in our despair. There is no limit to the hope Jesus is.

## *Action Step* 🚗

Three times this verse says, "he will deliver us." Pray a prayer of gratitude over the deliverance God has brought in your life.

## *Prayer*

Jesus, You are my hope. I know I can always count on You to deliver me from any peril working to take me down. Amen.

# Momming Is Tiring!

*Even youths shall faint and be weary, and young men shall fall exhausted; but they who wait for the LORD shall renew their strength; they shall mount up with wings like eagles; they shall run and not be weary; they shall walk and not faint.*
ISAIAH 40:30–31

Let's face it—being a mom is rewarding, but there is no tired like *mom* tired! We find innovative ways to grab a power nap whenever and wherever we can. We are master multitaskers. The weekends of our youth were spent getting home just before curfew, and now, moms are ecstatic to see Friday nights with only pajamas and an early bedtime planned. I now understand why my mother looked forward to the weekends.

Are you tired? Does the weight of the world feel heavy? Do you feel as though your strength is failing? I know it feels cumbersome in the world right now. Looking around can cause you to want to sneak back under the covers until it is all over. If you were honest, pressing on is taking a toll on you.

Isaiah is reminding us to wait in hope. Wait on the Lord through prayer and spending time in His presence. While in God's company, hope comes to the forefront. It is reignited and gives breath back to our lives.

God knew what was coming and was not caught off guard. He knows the end of the story, and the good news is we do too. We win!

## Action Step

If you are feeling tired, slow down to a walking speed while He renews your strength.

## Prayer

Thank You for being our living hope, Jesus! Revive my spirit as You renew my strength. Amen.

# Starting Something New

*For whoever has despised the day of small things shall rejoice,*
*and shall see the plumb line in the hand of Zerubbabel.*
ZECHARIAH 4:10

Do you ever find yourself falling in the trap of wanting to be where another mom is in her life? We see her middle and how God is moving, but we have no idea the valleys she faced in the beginning or the steps of faith it took for her to be where she is right now.

When I began writing, I had no idea what I was doing! I felt a bit like Sarah and laughed when God revealed to me what He wanted to birth through me. I learned quickly to not argue with the Lord—you will not win.

My beginning was a ten-day devotional titled *The Anxiety Elephants: 10-Day Devotional on Stomping Them Out*. My husband and I created it on our computer. I taught myself how to do the formatting. For hours, I searched for a free image of an elephant. With a tight budget, every penny mattered. I landed on a color pallet of orange-yellow with black and white writing. We had no idea what we were doing.

Without the beginning step, the middle and end will never happen.

What small beginning are you walking in right now? What have you been putting off or finally started? Have you taken a moment to rejoice with the Lord in these newfound steps?

God is rejoicing in your small beginning! How will you celebrate with Him?

## Action Step

What is your small beginning? Devise a plan to take this first step, and include your method of celebration!

## Prayer

God, I needed this reminder of the importance of the beginning. Where would we be without the beginning of creation or the birth of Jesus as man? As You celebrate my beginning, I am going to join in with You! Amen.

# Permission to Say "No"

*Bondservants, obey your earthly masters with fear and trembling, with a sincere heart, as you would Christ, not by the way of eye-service, as people-pleasers, but as bondservants of Christ, doing the will of God from the heart, rendering service with a good will as to the Lord and not to man.*
EPHESIANS 6:5–7

It is easy to get caught up in the people-pleasing game, isn't it? We apply this pressure on ourselves to make others happy because we are afraid of letting them down if we say *no*. What a relief to know the work we do should come from a heart desiring to please the Lord and not man.

There will always be a human around you who can never be pleased. Complaints will flow about everything you do and how things can be improved. There will always be someone who will be mad and point out negative things in the work you are doing. There will always be someone who will scoff at your *no*, even though it is said as a *yes* in obedience to God.

Others will not always approve of what God is telling you to do, and that is acceptable. The accolades of people do not get to define you. Surrendering all of who you are, to all of who He is, in every yes and no you give will characterize you as a true servant of the Lord.

This is your permission slip to say *no* to man and *yes* to God.

## Action Step

When you find yourself wanting to say *yes* to
make people happy, practice saying *no*.

## Prayer

Lord, set me free from the people-pleaser mentality.
I only desire to please You. Amen.

# The Jitters Have Taken Over

*Do not be anxious about anything, but in everything*
*by prayer and supplication with thanksgiving*
*let your requests be made known to God.*
PHILIPPIANS 4:6

First day of school jitters. New job jitters. Your children are having difficulty sleeping because of a stomachache thinking about their new classroom and teacher. Every time you close your eyes, your heartbeat pounds through your ear drums while your thoughts race to the What IFs of all the adjustments you are going to need to make with a shift in schedule. Your teenager comes into your bedroom crying with no explanation of what turned the spout on.

What is causing this anxiousness inside?

Anxiety can be paralyzing if we allow it to take over our bodies and minds. Hiding this normal struggle can increase its jitter-inducing power. Thoughts, feelings, change, trauma, memories, and experiences can all trigger the apprehension.

What is a faith-based practical response when these jitters move in? Paul gives us two specific steps to take when it comes to anxiousness. First, in everything, pray. He did not say, "In every big thing . . ." No. Paul makes it clear to talk to God about *all* the things, big and small. Pray about the anxiety you feel in your body and think in your mind. Be honest and ask God to help you shift out of this type of thinking and living. Finally, use thanksgiving. An attitude of gratitude is a natural built-in anxiety blocker. It keeps your brain from going to anxious places. When you look for items, experiences, and people to give thanks to God, you will experience a happy hormone hit. The jitters go away as the Lord brings peace.

## Action Step

Put your attitude of gratitude to work. Look for
as many things as possible for which to give God thanks.

## Prayer

God, thank You for allowing me freedom to talk
about my jitters with You. I want to take a minute
and thank You for (insert gratitude here). Amen.

# Stay in Your Lane

*"See that you fulfill the ministry that
you have received in the Lord."*
COLOSSIANS 4:17

Have you ever doubted the gifts or ministry God has given you? Do you look at others and compare yourself to them, deciding the Lord picked the wrong person? Are you afraid of what could happen if you do operate in your ministry and others decide to come out against you?

Stay in your lane and continue forward. Do not let doubt cause you to shift and merge into a lane you were never intended to go into. God has given you a ministry. Walk freely in this calling God has placed on you. You are being equipped to equip others.

Timothy can relate to what you are feeling. He was a timid guy being apprenticed by the apostle Paul. They had a close relationship, and Paul considered Timothy to be like a son. He wrote a letter to Timothy reminding him to fan into flame the gift of God on his life (2 Tim. 1:6–7). He was encouraging Timothy to keep going in his ministry.

Paul reminded Timothy that God gave him a ministry to put into action. This is the same for you. When we fan the flames, we increase the size and reach of the fire. The bigger it gets, the bigger the area it touches.

When you operate in the powerful spirit God has placed in you, the opinions of others will no longer hold you back. You will want to share the testimony the Lord has given you.

## Action Step 🥁

What does your ministry look like? Write a description below.

## Prayer

God, I realize the ministry and skills You have given me are not supposed to look like anyone else's. Help me to fan this flame to reach more souls for You. Amen.

# Breakfast on the Go

*All Scripture is breathed out by God and profitable for teaching, for reproof, for correction, and for training in righteousness, that the man of God may be complete, equipped for every good work.*
2 TIMOTHY 3:16–17

Breakfast is a must in our household. School mornings bring the most delicious early meal. Eggs and bacon are a favorite, with chocolate-chocolate chip muffins coming in as a close second. Yes, double the chocolate. Sunday mornings provide a different type of sustenance. Our daughters get to sleep a little later, so this morning meal is on the go. Breakfast is an important meal whether it is family gathered around the table or sticking it in a bag shaken in syrup. It provides us with fuel and energy.

God's Word provides in this same way to our souls. When we take the time to partake of it, we are armed with important teaching to help us navigate the day. It lights our path so we are aware of schemes against us. Scripture equips us in the same way protein gives our minds focus. God's Word points out what is true and what is a lie. Filling our minds with this manna will deliver sound doctrine to our thoughts.

Is there a specific way to read God's Word? Everyone will have their own preferred method. Some will choose to follow a plan to read the Bible in a year. Others will pick one book a month to dive in and dissect. Those who are new to discovering the Bible enjoy their start in the Gospels. Philippians is one of my favorite books to glean knowledge and encouragement. Whatever your plan is, stick to it and ask God to meet with you every time you open His Word.

## Action Step

Do you have a favorite way of reading the Bible?
Pick your plan and see how it goes!

## Prayer

I love Your Word, Lord! Thank You for providing living and active words for us to follow. Amen.

# Can I Run in the Race?

*Therefore, since we are surrounded by so great
a cloud of witnesses, let us also lay aside every weight,
and sin which clings so closely, and let us run
with endurance the race that is set before us.*
HEBREWS 12:1

Our elementary school PTO puts on a Shamrock Shuffle Run to raise funds for different programs we support every year. My oldest begged me to run in the one-mile fun run. Her friends were all doing it, and she did not want to miss out on this opportunity. One thing working against her was the lack of training she had. It wasn't actually a lack of training . . . it was zero training. To finish this fun run, she would have to endure hills, green color flying in the wind, and cold air hitting her in the face. When she turned the last corner, she was huffing and puffing through a leprechaun grin. She finished!

You have the race of *life* in front of you. There is a cloud of witnesses cheering you on here on earth and in heaven.

Endure. Stand strong in the battle of freeing your schedule of yeses, your mind of clutter, and time to grow in your relationship with Christ. It will not be easy, and there will be times you may want to fall into old habits. Ask the Holy Spirit to help you continue to walk in new ways you have been learning.

God will continue to reveal His truth in your yes to Him and His peace in your no to seeking the ways of the world.

## Action Step

Put an athletic pair of tennis shoes on today
as you focus on running the race of *life*.

## Prayer

Heavenly Father, give me endurance to finish this race. Amen.

# You Are Valuable

> *"Fear not, therefore; you are of*
> *more value than many sparrows."*
> MATTHEW 10:31

*You* are valuable.

I do not know where you find yourself as you read this simple but powerful truth. Are you sipping your morning coffee and wondering what you have to offer this world, thanks to fear? Do you find yourself with a puddle of tears gathering in your eyes while you wait for the afternoon line to move? Is the backdrop you see as you reflect on our Scripture the night sky filled with darkness as you question your worth?

In today's verse, Jesus is reminding the disciples of their worth to Him. He is driving the point home that we are precious in His sight. The very strands of hair on our heads are numbered because of the value we hold in His eyes.

The Lord wants the disciples to remember their value so the fear of being rejected by man will not hold them back from walking in their calling. They will never be rejected by God. Neither will you.

God placed a call on your life the moment you were created. He breathed value into you. Your *Abba* Father loves you and believes in you. He deemed your life worthy of Him dying for you long before you knew Him.

Fear does not have the authority to cancel the value God has already assigned to you. Knowing you cannot be devalued in the eyes of the Lord, how will you go out and live differently?

## *Action Step*

Face one fear today as you go out
in the God calling on your life.

## *Prayer*

Heavenly Father, Your love for me is more
than I can comprehend. I needed this
reminder that I am valuable. Amen.

# Morning Coffee

*And rising very early in the morning,*
*while it was still dark, he departed and went out*
*to a desolate place, and there he prayed.*
MARK 1:35

Nothing like a quiet morning. Silence sounds glorious. His Word jumps off the page and into our lives. God meets with us during this sweet juncture of time.

Why would it be valuable in this car line season to get up early and spend time with the Lord? Would it not be better to get a few more minutes of sleep and fit time with Jesus in later? I can relate to this question because I love my sleep . . . as I yawn typing this sentence.

When we get up early to talk with Jesus, it sets our day in motion. He speaks to our heart and shares nuggets of truth that will direct our path for the day. It is a time of uninterrupted listening on our part. Our priorities are kept in order when God comes first.

Follow the example of Jesus rising early. Try it for a few days. It takes time to make new habits stick. Push through the difficult beginning knowing the powerful presence awaiting you.

## Action Step 🥐

Time to get up! Create a plan and set your alarm to move your body out of the bed and seated before Jesus.

## Prayer

God, You know the mornings can be a struggle for me. Help me to get up and spend time in Your presence first. Amen.

# Motherhood in Such a Time as This

> *"For if you keep silent at this time, relief and deliverance will rise for the Jews from another place, but you and your father's house will perish. And who knows whether you have not come to the kingdom for such a time as this?"*
>
> ESTHER 4:14

"Why am I a mother in such a time of turmoil and division?"

Have you had this question, or one like it, plant into your head?

You have been placed in this season of motherhood for such a time as this. Yes, it is difficult and scary out there, but God chose you for right now . . . for this season . . . this time . . . this generation . . . these children. It was not a mistake. You are here for a reason.

It is easy to look around us and wonder what is going to happen to our kids. Why do they have to grow up in a world that seems further and further away from God? But all generations have gone through uncharted waters. Just as Esther stepped up with boldness, we must do the same.

Esther did not know what was going to happen when she went before the king. She knew that she had been placed in a position of power to save the Jews from annihilation. Staying silent was not an option for her.

We cannot stay silent on behalf of our children. I believe the deliverance that God has for this generation is waiting on us to speak.

Are you ready? Are you ready to stand firm in the face of a world that hates us? Are you ready to show your children what it looks like to follow Jesus no matter the cost? Are you ready to stand and fight for the ones God has entrusted in your care?

If your answer is yes, let's go together!

## Action Step

Take time to decide if you are ready to speak up
on behalf of your children.

## Prayer

I have really pondered this, Lord. I know You are calling me forth for such a time as this. Give me boldness to stand up and speak, fight, and pray on behalf of our children. Amen.

# Thank You

*Therefore, as you received Christ Jesus the Lord, so walk in him, rooted and built up in him and established in the faith, just as you were taught, abounding in thanksgiving.*
COLOSSIANS 2:6–7

We have not fully grasped the weapon God has given us through gratitude. A mind full of thankfulness leaves no place for fear, anxiety, or worrisome thoughts to linger. God gave us dopamine and serotonin in our brain as our feel-good hormones. He knew these components would be important in helping us to feel happy.

By being intentional with thankful thoughts, your brain remains in a calm state. Remaining in a place of thankfulness blocks fearful and panicked-filled beliefs.

If you were to challenge yourself over the next thirty days to think of three things you were thankful for, you might be surprised at how different you view life. By putting the practice of gratitude into motion, it retrains your brain to think differently. New pathways grow, opening your mind to see things through a brighter perspective.

God was so gracious to fill His Word with thanksgiving. He knew the power of being rooted in gratitude.

## Action Step

Are you up for the challenge? Start with seven days. Pick three new things you are thankful for every day.

## Prayer

God, You are amazing! You knew the power of thankfulness on our mind, body, and soul. Help me to live in this place of gratitude as I grow in my faith. Amen.

# Hiding in the Bathroom

*Behold, I am doing a new thing; now it springs forth,*
*do you not perceive it? I will make a way*
*in the wilderness and rivers in the desert.*
ISAIAH 43:19

I was hiding in the bathroom away from little hands, paws, and lists. I found my secret stash of chocolate and a Bible. Reading the Scripture from today, God began to peel back old layers I thought were gone. There were lingering beliefs and thought patterns holding on to my heart that were not healthy.

It is amazing the thinking that happens on a porcelain throne. The quiet echoes of lying thoughts were now flushed out by God with truth.

Do you find yourself hiding in unhealthy thought patterns? Has God revealed to you a new way of thinking and living that does not limit His power and authority in your life?

Letting go of this old way of living can be difficult. It feels familiar and safe. It also is pulling you away from the growth God wants to do in you. When we put a cap on what He can do in us and through us, we miss out on the limitless gifts He has.

It is scary to think and live in a new way, but with God, it is always worth it!

## Action Step

What is the limiting belief you want removed
from your life? Surrender it to the Lord, and ask Him
to help you think and believe in a new way.

## Prayer

Dear God, I am sorry I tried to put You in a limited box.
Thank You for reminding me that You are a
limitless God . . . not just for others, but for me. Amen.

# Friendship Seasons

> *Then Jonathan said to David, "Go in peace, because we*
> *have sworn both of us in the name of the LORD, saying,*
> *'The LORD shall be between me and you, and between my*
> *offspring and your offspring, forever.'" And he rose and*
> *departed, and Jonathan went into the city.*
>
> 1 SAMUEL 20:42

Car lines bring all sorts of friendships into our lives. They move from the years of toddler play dates to elementary school after-school outings to spend-the-night parties with friends in middle school. These friends will come and go just as you will enter and exit the lives of other mamas parked near you. This flow of companionship is not a bad thing; it is a part of how this season ebbs and flows. You spend a few years together and then move on. Some friendships, however, will withstand multiple hardships.

David and Jonathan had an interesting connection. Jonathan was in a tough spot because his father, Saul, was trying to kill David. These two friends made a covenant promise between one another. This relationship moved from these two being allies to protecting their children as well.

Do you have friends in your life who look out for your children? Do you do the same for them?

This type of companion is the one you want to cling to. Create an environment for this friendship to grow over time instead of being removed. Find space in your calendar to fellowship with this mama. This gathering could be over a meal, coffee, or buying groceries together. As you connect with one another, discover ways your children can do the same. Start a small group for your sons and daughters to grow in Christ with one another. Invite the other moms to help you direct this monthly meeting. Make time to do life together.

## *Action Step*

Reach out to the Jonathan in your life.
Set a date for the two of you to fellowship.

## *Prayer*

God, I want to thank You for the Jonathans You have
put in my life. Help us to lift one another up
as well as our children. Amen.

# I Have a Craving!

*The soul of the sluggard craves and gets nothing,*
*while the soul of the diligent is richly supplied.*
PROVERBS 13:4

A few years ago, my husband came to me with a craving for cheesecake. I was not surprised by this sweet request since this is his favorite dessert. It was close to our anniversary, so I thought I would find a recipe to attempt. Now, let's be clear . . . the recipe I searched for needed to have five ingredients or less. The importance of the fewest steps possible had top priority on this dessert journey. A no-bake option popped up in research, and I knew I had struck gold!

By diligently searching and putting the ingredients together, we were richly satisfied. If we had stopped at a craving, we would have missed out on a delicious work turning into something amazing!

Are you craving something different in your life but you have not taken any steps forward in making changes? Do you sense God is telling you to walk through a new door instead of wondering what it "might" lead to one day?

Take these daydreams and move them to reality steps. This movement will pave the way to what God is knitting inside of you to come to fruition.

## *Action Step* 🥟

Write down this new door God wants you to walk through.

## *Prayer*

Dear God, I am not quite sure what next steps
You would have me take. As You show me,
instill a diligent spirit in me to go for it. Amen.

# Our Daily Helper

*And hope does not put us to shame, because*
*God's love has been poured into our hearts through*
*the Holy Spirit who has been given to us.*
ROMANS 5:5

Kids love being the helper in a classroom setting. This gives them an opportunity to run errands for the teacher, do extra things on behalf of the class, and roam the hallways freely while their friends are doing math.

My daughters were always excited when their job for the week was Helper. They knew the teachers were counting on them to get certain tasks completed they could not do on their own.

When Jesus returned to heaven, He knew the same would be true for us. He was able to walk this earth with the disciples. Then He ascended back to His right-hand place by the Father's side. But that doesn't mean the two of them wanted to leave us alone. To continue to walk with us, the Father and the Son sent a Helper.

The Holy Spirit was sent to be our guide and our friend. He gives us the nudges we need to follow the ways of God. He convicts us if we begin to move in the wrong path. His method is not shame, but a voice filled with love to bring us back to what is best for our lives.

You can trust the Holy Spirit to lead and guide you just as you do God and Jesus. He is a person of the Trinity, after all. His existence helps us commune with, obey, and enjoy God in a way we could never do without Him.

Cry out to your Helper today. Get to know the Holy Spirit in a deeper way.

## Action Step

Have you ever talked to the Holy Spirit in your prayers? Give it a try today. It may feel awkward, but talk to Him just like you would Jesus.

## Prayer

Holy Spirit, I am grateful for Your presence in my life. Help me to walk in a holy manner. Amen.

# Remember When?

*And I looked and arose and said to the nobles and
to the officials and to the rest of the people, "Do not be
afraid of them. Remember the Lord, who is great and
awesome, and fight for your brothers, your sons,
your daughters, your wives, and your homes."*
NEHEMIAH 4:14

Recounting the goodness of God drives out fear-filled thoughts. It allows us to pull from strength and courage because we are not depending on ourselves but on the One who is great and awesome. If you were to take a moment right now, what are some things you remember God doing in your life only He could do?

I remember how God was with me as a six-year-old having surgery on my left foot. As the nurse wheeled me away from my earthly father, my heavenly Father never left my side. In the midst of those tears, He helped me know everything was going to be alright when I woke up.

I remember how God was with me in the darkest pit of depression and despair. His comforting arms were wrapped tight around me after hearing the word *miscarriage* and falling to the bottom of the bottom. He lifted my head and brought healing and restoration.

Nehemiah is reminding the Israelites that God is their best hope. He is on their side. Even though attacks are coming, they can continue building the wall knowing God is with them.

Remember how He has been with you. Remember how He loves you. Remember He is always the same, never changing. If He fought for you before, He will do it again.

## Action Step

Remember His awesome deeds in your life.

## Prayer

I want to take this time and recall all the good You have done in my life, Lord. I am where I am because of You. Amen.

# Speak Up

*O LORD, in the morning you hear my voice; in the morning
I prepare a sacrifice for you and watch.*
PSALM 5:3

When my children speak up and start a conversation with me, it does something to my insides. I feel an overwhelming amount of joy as I sit and listen to all they have to share. Some of their conversation is of no importance. Other details they slide in deal with matters of their heart and serious situations that happened in front of the lockers. I sit quietly as they share every piece they freely wish to give.

God loves it when we talk to Him. He wants us to come in His presence and sit with a heart full of words to share. He is ready to hear all that we have to divulge. Just as we sit with great anticipation when our kids invite us into the inner workings of their lives, so does our heavenly Papa.

David invites us into the practice of talking to God first thing in the morning, when we wake up. By doing first things first, we automatically shift our focus and trust to the Lord.

As the sun comes up, we can rise knowing our heavenly Father is leaning down listening for our voice. Incline into His presence. Open your mouth and reveal all you have been holding on to. God has all day to hear everything you are ready to release.

## Action Step

Talk to God about all the things. He is listening
with great anticipation.

## Prayer

To know that I can talk to You about everything, Lord, brings
me back to the truth of how much You love me. Get ready,
because I have a lot to share with You today. Amen.

# Look Out!

*Be sober-minded; be watchful. Your adversary the devil prowls*
*around like a roaring lion, seeking someone to devour.*
1 PETER 5:8

It was a quiet afternoon. Everyone was finding their place in line and enjoying the cool breeze from the fall season. The birds were singing, cows were mooing, and babies were crying. Everything seemed routine and normal.

*BOOM!*

For the first time in the history of car line, a wreck happened! I was looking down at my phone so I did not get to be a witness, but I did hear the aftershock. Both cars were bruised in the battle. The one in front, while following the flow of traffic, had stopped moving. The driver in the back had looked down for a swift second. This lack of attention for a brief moment changed everything.

Our enemy does not need long to take us down. He is on the hunt looking for the one person who has taken their eyes off the path for a few moments. Our eyes may wander to social media. Focus shifts off the Bible and on to reading the gossip of the day. He tickles our ears with messages doubting our purpose. He can manipulate situations in the blink of an eye if we are not prepared.

We must pay attention and always be aware of our surroundings. Satan does not play nice. He will use frustrating situations with our children, husbands, and friends to trip us up. Be prepared with Scripture to silence his lies. Lean on other believers to watch each other's back. Ask God to help you spot the wicked traps set for you to fall.

## Action Step

Write down our verse from today and put it where your entire family can see. Work together to stay alert against the enemy.

## Prayer

Lord, open my eyes to the trap of the enemy.
Keep my foot from slipping. Amen.

# Turn Up the Music, Mom!

*About midnight Paul and Silas were praying and singing hymns to God, and the prisoners were listening to them, and suddenly there was a great earthquake, so that the foundations of the prison were shaken. And immediately all the doors were opened, and everyone's bonds were unfastened.*

ACTS 16:25–26

When my kids were younger, they loved listening to loud music in the morning. We would roll the windows down, and they would yell at the top of their lungs, "Turn it up!" A Christian rap would greet us with a good morning, or a worship song we were learning to sing for church would play on repeat. As they got out of the car, the praises leaving their lips were weapons pelting the enemy.

Praise and worship are weapons God has given us to shift our focus to Him, our Problem Solver, and not the problem.

Can you imagine being in prison next to Paul and Silas when they began singing and praying after midnight? It was late and some of those men were probably tired and angry. As the tiredness wore off, they started listening to the hymns from two men refusing to allow their circumstances to dictate their trust in God. They used a song on their lips to get them through a horrible situation.

The unexpected takes place through an earthquake setting everyone free. Our praise and worship not only impacts our lives but the lives of others around us. Wielding our weapon of praise shuts down the plot of the enemy.

Worship is a powerful tool. It moves our perspective from seeing ourselves to seeing God in a deeper way. He is always worthy of our praise from a prison floor to a fancy room to the crumb-filled seat of your car.

## Action Step

Put your weapon of worship into action. Ask your kids to help you pick out praise and worship songs to listen to as you begin your car line routine.

## Prayer

You are worthy of all praise, Father! Amen and amen!

# Me? A Mom?

*"For nothing will be impossible with God."*
LUKE 1:37

Can you imagine being Mary? All of a sudden, an angel appears and tells you that you are going to birth the Savior of the world! Not only does he tell her that she is going to have a baby, but he informs her that Elizabeth, her cousin, is pregnant. This news is a big deal because Elizabeth was considered barren. This is the context from where our Scripture is coming from.

God birthed something impossible through Mary and Elizabeth when they became mamas. Both of their stories were different but filled with the miraculous work of God. Your story in becoming a mom is also a miracle. I do not know what the circumstances looked like around you, but holding your babies for the first time was a physical marker of incredible things taking place in your life that could only be done by God.

Impossible does not exist for Him. He can birth something through a barren womb. He can breathe life into a dead dream. He can take closed doors and open windows.

Mary gave us a beautiful example of how to not doubt and simply believe. Her response was not filled with questions trying to figure out how it would all happen. Faith took the place in the face of disbelief.

## Action Step

Where do you need to boldly say yes
to God in faith-filled belief?

## Prayer

You are the God who can do the impossible! I choose
to believe and trust in Your plan for me. Amen.

# You Don't Have to
# Be Perfect, Just Willing

*But immediately Jesus spoke to them, saying,*
*"Take heart; it is I. Do not be afraid." And Peter*
*answered him, "Lord, if it is you, command me to come*
*to you on the water." He said, "Come." So Peter got out*
*of the boat and walked on the water and came to Jesus.*
MATTHEW 14:27–29

One of the greatest miracles had just happened. The disciples watched Jesus use the lunch of a little boy feed over five thousand people. They observed Him break the bread and the fish, give thanks to the Father, feed everyone, and pick up twelve baskets full of leftovers.

Now they find themselves hanging out on a boat when a storm comes upon them. The waves are practically jumping in the boat. It is somewhere between 3:00–6:00 a.m. when they see this figure walking toward them on the water . . . have you ever seen anyone walking on water? Me neither!

It is Jesus! He is walking on the turbulent sea. Peter, who never finds himself lost for words, speaks up. I think I would have asked Jesus to get in the boat if I had been out there with them. We know from our Scripture that Peter goes all in! When Jesus told him to come, he did not hesitate and got out of the boat. For a moment, he experienced something no one else ever did. His feet stood and moved on top of the water toward Jesus.

But he took his eyes off the Lord and began to focus on the storm around him. As he started to sink in his mistake, he reached out to Jesus for help. Peter was not perfect. God gives us Peter as an example to realize we are not going to get it right all the time. The Lord knows this. He is not asking you to be the perfect mother. Mistakes are going to happen. All God asks of us is to be willing to grow in our surrender and trust in Him as the Lord molds us into the parents He calls us to be.

## Action Step

What area of parenthood have you not yet released to God? Release it into His hands.

## Prayer

God, I want to become the mom You created me to be. I know this requires daily surrender and obedience to Your plan. Help me grow in this way of living. Amen.

# I Gotta Go Potty

*Finally, be strong in the Lord and in the strength of
his might. Put on the whole armor of God, that you may
be able to stand against the schemes of the devil.*
EPHESIANS 6:10–11

Navigating car line days with toddlers can be adventurous. I will never forget the day I was picking my oldest up from first grade. My youngest was two at that time. We arrived to afternoon car line, and the dreaded proclamation no mama wants to hear moves through my car, "I gotta go potty, Mommy." We went through the whole song and dance before leaving the house. I asked her, like we do, multiple times if she needed to go potty. I made her sit on the potty . . . nothing. The forward motion of the car did something to her bladder.

I was trapped. I could not exit the line, and it was too late to check my daughter out of school and simply escape. I did what any good mom would do. I told her to hold it. Now, you can use your imagination at how well she received this command. Panic ensued and tears flowed . . . thankfully, only tears. The next thirty minutes were filled with songs, the I Spy game, and any story I could make up to get her mind off of the situation we were facing.

I was not prepared for a bathroom break. A plan of attack was missing from my parenting manual. It almost blew up in my face. This mistake reminded me of the importance of always being prepared for sneak attacks from the enemy. When we put the full armor on, we are being diligent and prepared for whatever battle will come our way.

## Action Step

Make a list of the armor of God. Place it in your car and daily recite putting it on.

## Prayer

God, help me to better prepare for sneak attacks from the enemy. Amen.

# Why Were You in Trouble?

*"I have said these things to you, that in me you
may have peace. In the world you will have tribulation.
But take heart; I have overcome the world."*
JOHN 16:33

You never want to drive up and see your child getting in trouble.
What felt like agonizing hours in the car line was only a mere
ten minutes as I watched my daughter sitting out of recess. It
was not typical of her to get in trouble, so this was startling to
see. She got in the car with her head held down as she told me
the situation. It dawned on me in that moment that trouble and
difficult times would continue to come her way . . . I wouldn't
be able to shield her from them. Instead, I could prepare her
to learn from them and to walk through them.

Jesus warned us that we would have troubles. He didn't
tell us that blessings would follow us day after day. He said we
*would* have trouble.

How do we take heart and walk through these dilemmas?

First, we hold on to the truth that Jesus has already won
the victory through death and resurrection. Then, we do not
allow difficult situations to stop us from moving forward. God
will be with us in the hard, so we must hold His hand and keep
stepping. Finally, we surrender our concerns and worries to
our heavenly Father. We are not robots. We are human with

emotions. It is important to name what we are feeling so it does not fester and grow.

Jesus gave us a warning with the good news that He had overcome the world. He gives us the ending so we can trust Him in the beginning and middle.

## Action Step

Describe how you will use these steps when trouble comes.

## Prayer

Jesus, You have overcome death, hell, and the grave! Help me to walk daily from this place of victory instead of defeat. Amen.

# Hearing Beauty in the Silence

*"Be still, and know that I am God. I will be exalted among the nations, I will be exalted in the earth!"*
PSALM 46:10

I turned off my car one day and rolled the windows all the way down. As the roar of the motor quieted, I heard silence. I looked around and saw two yellow butterflies dancing in the air. On the passenger side of the car, the sound of a birthday celebration rang up and down the street. A gentleman blew out his candles while sitting in his patio chair. In the rearview mirror, I saw a mom and teenage daughter laughing and dancing to a song I could not hear but one I knew was meaningful to them.

I looked around and saw beauty I would have missed had I stayed in the noise.

Have you ever found silence to be powerful? To sit in nothing can be a bit unnerving because you are left alone with your thoughts. But it can be moving because we are also left alone in the stillness of God's creation. In this powerful hush, we experience God's presence.

The Lord will use this serenity to show His glory. It is in these moments we are reminded who is fighting for us. The Creator of this universe chose us. He wanted a relationship with you and me. He invites us to go deeper in the stillness to get to know who He is.

## *Action Step* 🔅

It is time to get a little uncomfortable and be still. In the quiet, focus your heart on *who* God is, and allow His wonderful love to penetrate your soul to a deeper level.

## *Prayer*

Lord, I just want to be still in this moment with You. Amen.

# There's a Jungle in My Car

*For God is not a God of confusion but of peace.*
1 CORINTHIANS 14:33

I open the door and discover a treasure trove of water bottles balancing on top of each other in the backseat. As I peer through the driver's side window, I quickly become aware of the sweatshirts stacked haphazardly in the middle seat. Apparently, sweatshirts are a necessity even in sweltering temperatures. Finally, connecting all the clutter are stale snacks that were snuck out of lunchboxes but never completed. The jungle in my car is calling for a decluttering process.

What about our minds? Do you ever experience the clutter of negative thoughts bombarding you day after day? Do you sense overwhelming confusion? How do we declutter the pessimistic thoughts in our heads?

Journaling is a good practice. When you experience a bombardment of gloomy thoughts, grab a notebook and write them down as fast as they land. No one will see what you are writing, so free yourself from perfection in grammar and penmanship. Write until the thoughts stop. You can close the journal and put it away, or tear out the pages and throw them in the trash. One thing that has helped me in the past is crossing out the negative thoughts and writing over them with

God's truth. Holding on to sin and bitterness clogs our mind. Let go of any frustration or anxious thoughts.

By journaling and confessing, your mind and soul will feel like it got the detailed car wash. Time for a cleaning!

## Action Step

Start the process of journaling. If you do not have a notebook, grab a scrap piece of paper or a paper towel. Remove the negative thoughts, and replace them with God's truth.

## Prayer

God, it is time to clean up my mind. Help me to take the time to remove the gloom and doom from my thought process. Amen.

# I'm Sorry You Had a Bad Day

**_Jesus wept._**
JOHN 11:35

Not every day is going to feel like the best day ever. Nowhere in the Bible does it say to always be happy, always smile, and always have a cheery word to speak. You are going to have bad days. You may wake up one morning and experience a frustrating situation. You might come across a conversation that burns you inside with anger. You may get news no one wants to hear that brings you to your knees.

God gave us our emotions. We can look throughout the four Gospels and see Jesus experiencing all types of emotions. He felt righteous anger in the temple. Compassion for the hungry crowds. Sadness when His friend died. We have emotions. The key is to not allow them to have us.

By acknowledging what you are feeling, you are in control of them. When we deny what we are going through and experiencing internally, it allows them to grow. Sadness can move to dread. Anger can move to hatred. Frustration can lead to bitterness.

Don't give emotions an extended invitation to rule your life. If you have a bad day, recognize it and what all it brings. Through your sobbing and lamenting, talk to Jesus about your day. Take an Epsom salt bath and head to bed early. Begin again, knowing His mercy and grace are starting over with you.

## Action Step

Be honest about the day you are having. Acknowledge your emotions so they do not gain control over you.

## Prayer

Jesus, You gave me perfect examples of feeling
the emotions God has given. Help me to continue
following You in how I respond to my feelings. Amen.

# Don't Touch Your Sister

*Know this, my beloved brothers: let every person be quick to hear, slow to speak, slow to anger.*
JAMES 1:19

For some reason my kids love to get in one another's personal space in the afternoons and get their fingers close enough before the other one yells out as if a dagger has been thrown. I'm pretty sure I say, "Don't touch your sister," a million times a day. Isn't it amazing how long your arm becomes when you are crowned Mom? The flexibility that comes with this position is mind-boggling for the little ones who have not yet entered this field.

We can silence the arguments in our back seat with the snap of our fingers, but what do we do with confrontation that cannot be avoided or silenced with our "mommy sense"? How do we respond?

James gives us a simple plan, but we have to be intentional in its implementation. God gave us two ears and one mouth. He makes it very clear even in molding us together physically that listening is key to communication. When you find yourself facing confrontation, listen first. Put your two ears to work and ask the Lord to help you hear what you need to hear to diffuse the argument. After listening, be slow with what you allow to come out of your mouth.

Words are powerful and will stick forever. If they are life-giving, this is great news! However, if they are demeaning, it can take a long time to repair the hurt caused.

Listen carefully, speak slowly, and keep anger from seeping into the conversation. This game plan will help any difficult situation shift to open communication.

## Action Step

Practice listening more than talking this week in all of your conversations, and notice the difference.

## Prayer

Lord, help me to be quick to listen, slow to speak, and slow to anger. Amen.

DAY 90

# Driving, Driving, and More Driving

*I have fought the good fight, I have finished the race, I have kept the faith.*
2 TIMOTHY 4:7

There are days when the driving seems never-ending. You move through multiple lines in the morning from one side of the city to the other. Your afternoons double in the amount of time you sit and wait. From the waiting, you move to more hours of driving back and forth. You get one kid to practice, dropping the other one off after going back to school to get the homework that was forgotten. By the time everyone is to their set locations, it is time to begin the driving once more to pick everyone up and get home for dinner, bath, and bed.

The driving matters. The work matters. It feels monotonous, but keep driving. When you move from mile marker to mile marker, you are waging war against the enemy. Fight the battle in the spirit over their minds and souls. Keep waging war against the enemy while you sit in lines.

Be the taxi and the warden when needed. Roll the windows down, and turn the worship music up. Cry tears of lament and believe with passionate faith in the plan God has for your road warriors.

This car line race is more of a marathon than a sprint. We can outlast the enemy by clinging to our faith in what God has in store for them.

> Keep driving when it feels hard.
>
> Keep driving when it becomes frustrating.
>
> Keep driving when they ask you at the last minute.
>
> Keep driving every opportunity that comes.

No matter what, keep driving.

## Action Step

Pray as you drive today.

## Prayer

Lord, I do not want to lose sight of the importance of this season. As I drive, protect these children and build them up to stand firm against their enemy. Amen.

# Test Today?

*Count it all joy, my brothers, when you meet trials of various kinds, for you know that the testing of your faith produces steadfastness. And let steadfastness have its full effect, that you may be perfect and complete, lacking in nothing.*

JAMES 1:2–4

Does the dread of taking a test ever go away? I will never forget taking my driver's license test. I practiced for months. Coming to a complete stop was a specialty of mine. Doing a three-point turn was a breeze. The day of the test did not make me feel warm and fuzzy inside. My brain went into overdrive and wanted to escape the situation. As we entered the vehicle, my instructor told me to turn left. I put my left blinker on, and my brain said, "*Run!*" The tires were turning right, and we were merging onto the busy highway. We both cried, and I am pretty certain the fear of death was in her eyes. Needless to say, she failed me. Grace swooped me up and gave me one more opportunity that day to retake the test. I passed!

The first test prepared me for what I would face later on.

Trials and testing are not fun, but they are not intended to be. God uses them to grow the roots of our faith strong. Going through difficult situations teaches us how to respond with unwavering faith. If it does falter, the Lord will use that experience to open our eyes up to doing it differently the next time.

Each test adds a new layer of endurance to our faith walk. If it were always easy, we would run away from the enemy versus standing strong and facing him.

Are you walking through a test right now? Praise the Lord! He will use this trial to draw you near to Him as your endurance and courage muscles grow!

## Action Step

Do you remember a time in your life when you failed a test and it helped you in the long run? Write this memory down.

## Prayer

God, this test is not easy, but I rejoice in how You are using it to grow endurance in my relationship with You. Amen.

# Pizza Night

*Trouble and anguish have found me out,*
*but your commandments are my delight.*
PSALM 119:143

"Don't panic!" This was a favorite saying from my high school teacher and our school's football coach. He would yell this out at random times during tests, and we would get tickled while trying to choose the correct answer. This man is no longer here with us on earth, but his words still ring through the air.

These two words may have been spoken to you at different times. As much as this phrase is meant to help, it does the opposite. Panic ensues and stress is felt throughout your body and home.

We all experience stress, but how do we keep this anguish from stealing from our life? Sometimes, you just have to order the pizza. When you have an increased load, kids have tests to take, and you know something inside is about to explode, simplifying something like dinner can diffuse the bomb.

Pausing and turning our thoughts to the Lord will help us move out of this emotional state and into a place of rational thinking. If we make decisions or say things out of this emotional place, we tend to regret it. Use this healthy halt while eating your pepperoni and cheese.

## *Action Step* 🌮

Order the pizza!

## *Prayer*

Dear Lord, keeping it simple will help me keep my thoughts
focused on You and not being controlled by my emotions.
Amen.

# I Love You

*The LORD appeared to him from far away.*
*I have loved you with an everlasting love;*
*therefore I have continued my faithfulness to you.*
JEREMIAH 31:3

For the mom who feels unlovable, He sees you from afar.

There was a time in my life I felt unlovable as a young mom. I was filled with depression, anxiety, fear, and shame. I found myself in a cascade of negative emotions flowing over me telling me how I was failing my child and not worthy of the love of our heavenly Father.

When school days came around, I would tear up thinking the teachers would do a much better job of helping her learn and be loved. I would drive away with my head hung in defeat before the speedometer crested 30 mph. For weeks I battled this anguish. My heart became fragile and soon cracked under the pressure of trying to be "fine."

Far away, whispers were flickering in my soul. A calling of hope emerged and reminded me of God's faithfulness.

He loves you, and He is whispering in a gentle and inviting voice today: *I love you.*

## *Action Step* 🌮

Do a quick search for some encouraging verses
focused on God's everlasting love for you.
Write them down on index cards, placing them in your car,
under your pillow, bathroom mirror, and refrigerator to keep
this much-needed reminder in front of you.

## *Prayer*

Heavenly Father, you knew how much I would need the
reminder of your everlasting love. Help me to abide in this
truth when shame tries to cause doubt to cloud my thinking.
Amen.

# I'm *Just* a . . .

*Now when they saw the boldness of Peter and John, and perceived that they were uneducated, common men, they were astonished. And they recognized that they had been with Jesus.*
ACTS 4:13

Most moms will describe themselves using a familiar statement: *I'm just a mom.* Have those words ever tripped out of your lips?

You are not *just* a mom . . . You *are* a mom. You are making the most of moments in your time with the Lord and your family.

Would you tell your closest friend she is *just* a mom? If you would not slam this insult on her, why are you attaching it to yourself? What would you tell your bestie who is struggling with thinking she is *"just . . . ?"*

A few encouraging words you might say to her would look like this:

- You are doing better than you think you are.
- God has not brought you this far to leave you by yourself.
- God specializes in using common people to do uncommon things.

- God does not need a list of your lack of qualifications; He called you so He will equip you.

Take a moment and read this list again over yourself. Let these statements erase any "just" trying to demean you.

Describing Peter and John as uneducated, common men would not be words you and I would have used. *Just* ordinary males is how the people around them viewed their lives. What set these two apart is the relationship they had with Christ. The more time you spend at the feet of Jesus, the more His extraordinary work is revealed.

## *Action Step*

Remove "just" from your description.

## *Prayer*

God, forgive me for belittling myself. Your specialty is using ordinary people to do extraordinary things. Amen.

# Go

> *"Go therefore and make disciples of all nations, baptizing them in the name of the Father and of the Son and of the Holy Spirit, teaching them to observe all that I have commanded you. And behold, I am with you always, to the end of the age."*
>
> MATTHEW 28:19–20

God wants to use us to make disciples of the young ones He has placed under our wings. The command of *go* is one that can take place beneath our own roof. The enemy is after this generation, and yet God saw fit to place you here and now to be a reservoir to pour His light and love through the children in your care.

They are never too young or too old to train up. Discipleship happens by being an example. Dive deeper into the Bible together. Be a guide to them in how to read the Word and apply it to every area of life. Model sharing the Good News in front of your teens and tweens. Make corporate worship a priority for your family. Demonstrate the importance of honoring God in all you do from the music you play in your car to the way you treat others. Do not hide the struggles and difficulties, but show them how to turn to God in challenging times for answers rather than to popular search engines.

*Go* into your car every day knowing His salvation could take place at any moment. Be prepared for the move of the

Holy Spirit. As you follow the command to be a witness to all nations, remember this includes the tiny world right next to you.

## Action Step

Pray together as a family before bedtime. Ask God to reveal new ways He wants you to disciple your children.

## Prayer

God, guide me in the ways You would have me disciple these children. Help me to be obedient in living a life that brings glory to You in front of them. Amen.

# Did Somebody Say *Change*?

*And being warned in a dream not to return to Herod, they*
*departed to their own country by another way.*
MATTHEW 2:12

How do you respond when *change* comes into your life?

At our elementary school, each grade has a specific spot for afternoon pick-up. You get used to one location, and *bam*—the next year it's time for a change. You learn a new direction, a new path, and a new way.

I can remember facing change when my husband and I were newly married. We moved back to his hometown so he could start his own business. The change of moving from one town to another a few years later took place. It was a good adjustment, but hard.

Mary and Joseph had a plan, a route to travel, and God called out to Joseph to make a switch.

When He brings change in our lives it is not to hurt us, but to help us and protect us. He knew more about the situation going on around Mary and Joseph and the schemes that Herod had created, and God's plan was much greater than their adversary.

Instead of asking why God is bringing change, what if we ask some different questions: How do you want me to seek

You, Lord, in this change? How do I need to trust You? What are You revealing in this change?

By shifting your inquiry, the new developments God is performing in your life will ground you in a place of trust instead of the slippery slope of doubt.

## Action Step

Just for fun, change one thing in your routine.

## Prayer

God, even though change is hard for me, I want to trust when You allow for these new shifts to come in my life. Amen.

# How to Wait in Line and on God

*Meanwhile all Judah stood before the LORD, with their little ones, their wives, and their children.*
2 CHRONICLES 20:13

What type of "waiter" are you? I don't mean someone serving sweet tea at your favorite restaurant. When I say *waiter*, I am referring to how you wait in the car line.

There are those who are the *long waiters*. You make sure your arrival is one of the firsts, if not first, in line. You have a bag packed with reading material, snacks, and maybe even exercises you can do from the waist up.

Then, there are those of us who are the *activity waiters*. We arrive in line early, not because we want to be first, but because we have places to get to and practices to get done. We also have a snack bag, but it is not for us. It's for the scavengers we are picking up to bring to their next drop-off.

Finally, there are those of you who I am slightly jealous of. You are the *no waiters*. You arrive just in time to pull in at the last minute. You come in on two wheels, and the line is moving and progressing with ease. Your kids know you will be last and have come to terms with it.

How do you feel about waiting on the Lord? Do you find at times you get frustrated if God is not moving at the pace you would like? Do you wonder why He doesn't have the snack bag filled and waiting on you to come to Him?

I look at the example King Jehoshaphat gives us. He was surrounded by an enemy on all sides. Our Scripture shows us that he gathered everyone together to pray and fast.

Then, they waited. They waited on the Lord to answer.

God answered with encouragement and hope. He reminded them the battle was His and they could trust as they stood and waited.

Resolve in your heart to seek the Lord in your waiting. Be honest with Him in your prayers and tell Him you don't know what to do, but you are choosing to put your eyes on Him. Then praise while you wait.

## Action Step

Practice waiting on the Lord. Seek Him, pray, and praise.

## Prayer

Dear Lord, I confess I have difficulty waiting on You.
I choose to resolve my heart toward Your face and
praise You as I learn to halt in Your presence. Amen.

# No One Warned Me about This Part

*And I am sure of this, that he who began a good work in you*
*will bring it to completion at the day of Jesus Christ.*
PHILIPPIANS 1:6

No one gives you a warning about all the emotions and feelings you experience driving through the car line. Watching your children exit the car for the first time and not looking back as though they need you to tell them when to breathe and which direction to turn.

No one gives you a heads-up for the last day you drop them off in car line as they await the faithful day of getting their driver's license and assume the responsibility for their route to school and all their activities.

How do we let go of control and not get eaten alive by anxiety? This is the point where we must recognize a hard truth: we never really were in control and they were never really ours. They have always been the Lord's on loan to us.

That one hurts even as I type it. We can trust that He will complete His work in their lives, but we also must remember that He is doing a work in us. As you go through each car line and each phase, God is pulling another layer off of you and putting another layer of Himself on you. He is molding you into everything that He had in mind when He created you.

Your life is not over when the taxi service is no longer needed. It takes a turn into a new area of work needed to be done. God is just getting started in this new phase. Trust Him to complete it.

## Action Step

Identify where you are currently in this phase of work.
Ask the Lord to continue to remove a layer of you
as He puts on a new layer of Himself.

## Prayer

God, I lay down all my anxieties. I was never meant
to control all the things. I am releasing the controls
and trusting that the work You are doing will come to
completion in my life and my children's lives. Amen.

# The Glory Days

*Set your minds on things that are above, not on things that are on earth. For you have died, and your life is hidden with Christ in God. When Christ who is your life appears, then you also will appear with him in glory.*
COLOSSIANS 3:2–4

There are moments when you are rushing to the car line to have a quick respite before the chaos ensues. On those days, you turn the car radio up, and a blast from the past sings through your speakers. All of a sudden, the glory days fill your car as you go back to the last prom dance with your ex-boyfriend you just knew you were going to marry.

Or, you find yourself entering a time machine with a rap song you and your friends knew by heart and gave it all you had, holding your hair brushes and mixing spoons, laughing in the mirror.

For a fleeting second, you go back to your glory days and remember the joyous occasions you experienced and the moments you thought were life-altering. Reliving the grandeur of the past is fun, but as Christians we have glory days to look forward to.

God's Word reminds us that this earth is not our home and heaven is waiting on us.

Can you imagine walking the streets of gold, seeing your grandparents and friends who have already gone on before us, and hearing the cries of "Holy, Holy, Holy is the Lord God Almighty!"

There is so much ahead for us that we cannot wrap our brains around. Pause and take time to think about what God has in store. There will be no more pain or weeping. Turmoil will no longer plague our streets.

When the tension of this world appears unbearable, hold on to the hope you have to look forward to. The glory days of your past won't hold a candle to the glory days to come forever with King Jesus.

## Action Step

Imagine what it will be like in our eternal, heavenly home.

## Prayer

Dear Jesus, it's hard to fathom what heaven will be like, but I praise You with great anticipation knowing this is not my home. Being with You forever one day is a glory day I look forward to! Amen.

# I *Love* Car Line!

*There is nothing better for a person than that*
*he should eat and drink and find enjoyment in his toil.*
*This also, I saw, is from the hand of God.*
ECCLESIASTES 2:24

"I love car line!"

As these words jumped out of my teenager's mouth, my feet cemented to the floor in shock. Without hesitation I responded back with, "You *what*?!" With the biggest grin I have ever seen on a Tuesday morning, she told me how much she missed talking to her friends in the afternoon because of a practice she normally had to go to. Today, she got the time back she had been missing.

God began to chisel the hardness away in my heart around the thought of car line through the help of the Holy Spirit. He showed me this toil given to me was a gift and that the moments were fleeting. It took a teenager's enthusiasm over simple conversations to remind me how important this job is in this season.

I get it . . . the car line life is not always easy, and the work some days feels like a never-ending pilgrimage.

Instead of wishing this pathway away, let's task one another to find a way to enjoy it. In a few short years, we may be begging for the long lines, busy schedules, and never-ending, "Mom, can you take me . . ." requests.

This is a work given to us by God. Look at the hard moments through a lens of joy. See the long lines with a new anticipation of the life-changing conversations that could happen in the passenger seat. Till the ground and plant seeds of *truth* as the backpacks go on and tiny hands let go of yours.

Don't stop praying with your mama tears. Armor up and remind your enemy that car line moms are not the ones to mess with on a Monday morning.

Enjoy the moments. Make the most of them. See them. Feel them. Be present in them. Fall in love with this season recognizing God is doing a work in you and through you. In the coming and the going, look to Him.

## Action Step 🥐

Write, "I Love Car Line" on a piece of paper and place it on your dashboard. Use this as a reminder to be present in this short, but powerful season God has given you.

## Prayer

God, I want to proclaim my new love for the car line life! Thank You for this opportunity to raise up this generation. Mold me as You mold them. Amen.

# Want more?
# Check out these
# bestselling devotionals
# from B&H.